HIDDEN HISTORY
— OF —
KENTUCKY
IN THE CIVIL WAR
BERRY CRAIG

THE
History
PRESS

Published by The History Press
Charleston, SC 29403
www.historypress.net

Copyright © 2010 by Berry Craig
All rights reserved

First published 2010
Second printing 2011
Third printing 2012
Fourth printing 2013

Manufactured in the United States

ISBN 978.1.59629.853.8

Library of Congress Cataloging-in-Publication Data

Craig, Berry.
Hidden history of Kentucky in the Civil War / Berry Craig.
p. cm.
ISBN 978-1-59629-853-8
1. Kentucky--History--Civil War, 1861-1865--Anecdotes. 2. United States--History--
Civil War, 1861-1865--Anecdotes. 3. Kentucky--Biography--Anecdotes. I. Title.
E509.C735 2010
976.9'03--dc22
2010003089

To Professor Roy O. Hatton of Murray State University, my mentor and a student of T. Harry Williams, and to his late wife, Marjorie Hatton, who always laughed at my jokes.

Contents

Introduction

Divided We Stood

U nited We Stand, Divided We Fall" is Kentucky's motto. Yet the Civil War sharply split the Bluegrass State.

Kentucky natives headed the Union and Confederate governments. President Abraham Lincoln, the sixteenth president of the United States, was born near Hodgenville in 1809. Jefferson Davis, the Confederacy's only president, was born in Fairview the year before.

Kentucky did not secede from the Union and join the Confederacy. Nonetheless, Kentucky had a star on both the American and Confederate flags. Some secessionists created their own Confederate state "government." Dubious as the action was, it was enough to get Kentucky "admitted" as the thirteenth Confederate "state." (Missouri, a border slave state like Kentucky, also had a rump Rebel "government" and was the twelfth Confederate "state.")

Kentucky furnished between 90,000 and 100,000 men to the Union side. Another 25,000 to 40,000 Kentuckians joined in the Confederate forces, according to *A New History of Kentucky* by Lowell H. Harrison and James C. Klotter. The Union total includes more than 23,700 African Americans. Only Louisiana furnished more black troops to the Union military than Kentucky did.

Probably every Kentucky county supplied men to both sides, though the ratios varied. Most Kentucky counties sent more men north than south.

Above, left: President Abraham Lincoln. *Courtesy of the Kentucky Historical Society.*

Above, right: President Jefferson Davis. *Courtesy of the Kentucky Historical Society.*

But some counties gave almost equal numbers of soldiers to the Union and the Confederacy.

The war sundered many Kentucky families, from the humblest to the richest and most powerful. Breckinridge, Clay and Crittenden men were found in Union blue and Confederate gray. Even First Lady Mary Todd Lincoln had Rebel relatives in her native Kentucky—her half sister was married to Confederate General Ben Hardin Helm.

Kentuckians fought Kentuckians in some of the bloodiest battles of America's bloodiest war. The names and faces of the winning and losing generals of those battles are in most history books.

But this book is not like most history books. It is about hidden history. Most of these stories are not found in other history books. Some of them are proof that the Civil War was truly "a brother's war" in the home state of Lincoln and Davis.

Divided we stood.

Part I

1860–1861

"An Infernal Old Jackass"

No son of Kentucky is more famous or more revered than Abraham Lincoln, and rightly so.

His birthplace close to Hodgenville, the Larue County seat, is a national shrine. Lincoln's statue stands tall in the capitol rotunda in Frankfort.

However, no president lost an election in Kentucky by a wider margin than did the Great Emancipator. When he ran in 1860, Lincoln got less than 1 percent of the vote.

No president, while in office, was more unpopular in the Bluegrass State than was Lincoln. "People are amazed when I tell them what most Kentuckians really thought of Lincoln," said historian and writer Ron Bryant, manager at Waveland State Historic Site in Lexington. "Lincoln and the Republicans opposed slavery. Kentucky was a slave state."

Kentuckians reviled Lincoln from Paducah to Pikeville. In one letter, a young hothead from Lexington called the president "an infernal old Jackass," according to *Lincoln and the Bluegrass: Slavery and Civil War in Kentucky* by William H. Townsend. "I should relish his groans and agonies if I could see him put to torture in hell or anywhere else," the youth added. "He has chosen to become the representative of the Republican Party and as such I should like to hang him."

According to Townsend, the *Lexington Kentucky Statesman* charged that Lincoln was afraid to visit his native state because voters would "catch him, tar and feather him, and set him on fire to make a torch-light procession of him."

In 1860, John Bell, candidate of the Constitutional Union Party, earned Kentucky's dozen electoral votes. He collected 66,051 ballots to 53,143 for John C. Breckinridge of Lexington, the southern Democrat, and 25,638 for northern Democrat Stephen A. Douglas, according to *Presidential Politics in Kentucky, 1824–1948* by Jasper B. Shannon and Ruth McQuown. Lincoln's total was 1,364, the authors added.

Lincoln won a second term in 1864, running on the Union ticket. He lost Kentucky again but fared better in the Bluegrass State, carrying 25 of 101 counties that posted returns. Even so, Democrat George B. McClellan outpolled Lincoln 64,301 to 27,787. Kentucky thus gave the president "the lowest vote [he]…received in any of the 25 states which participated in the balloting," Shannon and McQuown wrote.

Lincoln, one of America's greatest presidents, became popular in Kentucky only after he was assassinated in 1865, according to Bryant. Other historians agree.

"A great transformation seems almost mysteriously to have swept over the people when the word came that Lincoln was dead," wrote E. Merton Coulter in *The Civil War and Readjustment in Kentucky*. "From their customary attitude of condemnation and vilification, they now turned to honoring and praising."

"THE CONFEDERACY OF PORTLAND"

Here's a Civil War history quiz. Which seceded first?

A. South Carolina.

B. Louisville's Portland neighborhood.

If you answered B, go to the head of the class. "Portland's always had an independent streak," said Tom Owen, a University of Louisville archivist and historian. Tiny Portland "seceded" from Louisville on December 13–14, 1860. South Carolina left the Union on December 20.

Portland's secession was a prank, according to Robert Emmett McDowell's book *City of Conflict: Louisville in the Civil War 1861–1865*. "The joke ceased to be funny when news of actual secession burst like a bomb on the city a week later," the author added.

Apparently, some Portlanders were never happy with their community's merger with larger Louisville. "Portland…seceded from Louisville with whoops of derision," according to McDowell. He added that Portland "delegates" gathered "at Fred Duckwall's saloon on the night of December 13 and…proclaimed the Confederacy of Portland." A "formal 'Declaration of Independence'" was to happen "early after lunch" on December 14.

Meanwhile, the Portlanders hoped that Butchertown would come into the confederacy. They knew the Point was with them, McDowell also wrote.

The delegates duly drew up a preamble and resolutions of independence, aimed at making "Portland…perfectly independent of all the nations of the world." More "resolutions laid claim to one-half the Jefferson County Courthouse and other public buildings and property throughout the city, and stated that 'we do not care if Shippingport joins us or not,'" according to *City of Conflict*.

The confederacy's flag was to be "two cat-fish, *Saltant*, on a market stall for a background," McDowell wrote. Because the Portland secessionists met at a local watering hole, they may have been "moved by the spirit—or spirits—of the day," he suggested.

"A VERY DELICATE QUESTION IS ARISING AS TO WESTERN KY"

If Tennessee hadn't seceded from the Union, Kentucky's Jackson Purchase region might have become part of a new Confederate state, according to a state historical marker on the court square in Mayfield.

The olive-green metal plaque notes that in May 1861 representatives from the Purchase—the state's westernmost region—and from twenty west Tennessee counties convened in the Graves County seat, where they expressed "belief in Southern cause, dissatisfaction with Kentucky adherence to Union and Tennessee delay joining South." Consequently, they voted "to secede and form a Confederate State," the plaque claims, adding, "with Tennessee's vote to secede, June 8, 1861, proposal abandoned."

The sign is not quite right. Delegates to the Mayfield convention, which met on May 29–31, only talked about secession. But that made the conclave unique. The Purchase was evidently the only section of a loyal state that flirted with joining the Confederacy on its own.

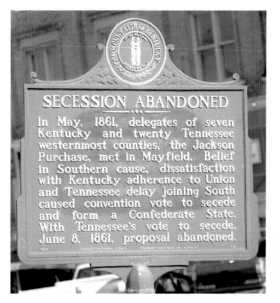

A state historical marker tells us about the all-but-unknown convention at which western Kentucky secession was discussed. *Photo by the author.*

Representative Henry C. Burnett. *Courtesy of the Library of Congress.*

The gathering alarmed Kentucky Unionists. George D. Prentice, sharp-penned editor of the pro-Union *Louisville Journal*, warned that the Mayfield convention was a dastardly plot to split the state. Loyal Kentuckians would not stand for it, he thundered.

The convention also grabbed headlines as far away as New York. President Lincoln heard about the Mayfield meeting, too. On May 30, General George B. McClellan wrote Lincoln from Cincinnati that "a very delicate question" was "arising as to Western Ky—that portion west of the Tenna. River."

In the letter, which is located in the Lincoln Papers in the Library of Congress, McClellan said that he was sending U.S. Navy Lieutenant (and future Union general) William O. Nelson, a leading Kentucky Unionist, to "explain to you that a convention is now being held at Mayfield which may declare that the 'Jackson Purchase' separate from Ky, its annexation to Tenna, & that this will be followed by an advance of Tenna. troops upon Columbus & Paducah."

Apparently, official records of the convention do not survive. Ironically, the only known eyewitness account is that of J.N. Beadles, a Mayfield Unionist who somehow managed to view the proceedings. The *Journal* of June 6 published his version of what happened. So did the *New York Tribune* four days later.

Reportedly, 3,500 spectators watched the convention, which met at the courthouse with 155 to 160 delegates present. "Such a scene of juggling, and wireworking, and private caucusing I never witnessed before," Beadles wrote. He claimed that after secession was debated the delegates rejected the idea because they were convinced that Kentucky was bound to secede. They were wrong.

Kentucky was neutral in May 1861. Most Kentuckians favored neutrality, just as they would support the Bluegrass State's forthright declaration for the Union in September 1861.

On the other hand, the Purchase remained resolutely Rebel to the end of the war. The Purchase—Ballard, Carlisle, Calloway, Fulton, Graves, Hickman, Marshall and McCracken Counties—was Kentucky's only Rebel-majority region.

The Purchase was dubbed "the South Carolina of Kentucky" for its Southern leanings. Paducah, the region's largest town, was so pro-Confederate that it was nicknamed "the Charleston of Kentucky."

Confederate records indicate that between 5,000 and 5,500 Purchase men volunteered for the Confederate forces. A March 1, 1865 report from the state adjutant general credited the Purchase with 650 white Union enlistments and 251 African American enlistments though December 31, 1864. (There would have been few Union or Confederate enrollees in Kentucky after that date.)

"The Blood of These Hessians Would Poison the Most Degraded Tumble Bug in Creation"

Yankees weren't just the enemy to Len G. Faxon, editor of the *Columbus Crescent*. They were "bow-legged, wooden shoed, sour craut stinking, Bologna sausage eating, hen roost robbing Dutch sons of ---." Their commander was a thieving, lying lush who "embodied the leprous rascalities of the world" and deserved to be hanged.

Objectivity was not a hallmark of Civil War journalism on either side. Vitriol and vilification were the stock in trade of editors and reporters, North and South. But few verbal broadsides were as withering as Faxon's 1861 blast in the *Crescent*.

It even amazed the "world's first and greatest" war correspondent, Sir William Howard Russell of the *London Times*. Russell preserved Faxon's fulminations in *My Diary North and South*, his American Civil War journal.

Faxon might have been Kentucky's most Southern-sympathizing editor. But there is no doubt that he spoke for most of his readers. Few Kentucky towns were more pro-Confederate than Columbus, a Mississippi River port in Hickman County. The nearby Yankees knew it.

Shortly after the war started, Union troops occupied Cairo, Illinois, at the confluence of the Ohio and Mississippi Rivers. The post commander, Colonel Benjamin Prentiss, suspected that citizens of Columbus were spying on his troops and trading with the Confederate enemy. Checked by Kentucky neutrality, though, Prentiss kept his soldiers away.

Still, he kept a wary eye on the town, with its one-hundred-foot dirt bluffs from which an army could command the river for miles around. Prentiss also knew that Confederate troops were poised at Union City, Tennessee, only twenty-five miles south of Columbus. Most Columbus citizens hoped that the Rebels would save them from the Yankees.

Knowing that the Confederates were close, Prentiss regularly sent armed steamboats to patrol the Mississippi. On June 12, 1861, he ordered the armed steamboat *City of Alton* to scout the river to Columbus and below. Union infantry were aboard.

The boatload of bluecoats spotted no Rebels, but Yankee hackles rose when the soldiers spied a big Confederate flag flying over Columbus. The *City of Alton* mysteriously developed engine trouble and headed toward the town landing.

Down clattered the wooden gangplank. Musket-toting troops scrambled ashore, led by Colonel Dick Oglesby, an Illinoisan who would become a general, governor and United States senator. The Northern soldiers eagerly tore down the enemy banner, claiming themselves a war trophy.

Pro-Southern Columbus citizens shot only dirty looks at the unwelcome visitors. But a man defiantly told the *Alton*'s skipper that "Columbus is all right for the South," according to the *Memphis Appeal*. A plucky patriot woman promised that "she had enough material to make another flag of the same description, and that it would be flying before sundown." (According to legend, a local wag ran women's underwear up the flagpole.)

Had it not been for Russell, Faxon's fusillade might have been forgotten. No copies of the 1861 *Crescent* are known to survive. Russell, who had reported on the Indian Mutiny and the Crimean War, was in the Union camp at Cairo when he got a copy of the *Crescent* with Faxon's version of the flag snatching.

Apparently, Faxon was away in the Confederate army and missed the flagnapping. Russell called him "Colonel L.G. Faxon of the Tennessee Tigers." In any event, he soon returned to town. He opened fire in the June 19 *Crescent*, in which he also apologized "for the non-appearance of the journal for several weeks," according to Russell.

Russell quoted Faxon's wish that the folds of the flag "had contained 1000 asps to sting 1000 Dutchmen to eternity unshriven." The Yankees probably would have been too besotted to feel it, according to the editor:

> *The mosquitoes of Cairo have been sucking the lager-bier out of the dirty soldiers there so long, they are bloated and swelled up as large as spring 'possums. An assortment of Columbus mosquitoes went up there the other day to suck some, but as they have not returned, the probability is that they went off with* delirium tremens; *in fact, the blood of these Hessians would poison the most degraded tumble bug in creation.*

With that, Faxon reloaded and fired again:

> *When the bow-legged wooden shoed, sour craut stinking, Bologna sausage eating, hen roost robbing Dutch sons of --- had accomplished the brilliant feat of taking down the Secession flag on the river bank, they were pointed to another flag of the same sort which their guns did not cover, flying gloriously and defiantly, and dared yea! double big black dog-dared, as we used to say at school, to take that flag down.*

The Yankees declined, Faxon claimed. "The cowardly pups, the thieving sheep dogs, the sneaking skunks, dare not do so, because their twelve pieces of artillery were not bearing on it."

After flaying the Federal soldiers, Faxon lambasted their leader Prentiss, a tough-as-boot-leather soldier who would make general and become a Union hero at the Battle of Shiloh in April 1862. Faxon dismissed him as

> *a miserable hound, a dirty dog, a sociable fellow, a treacherous villain, a notorious thief, a lying blackguard, who has served his regular five years in the Penitentiary and keeps his hide continually full of Cincinnati whiskey, which he buys by the barrel in order to save his money—in him are embodied the leprous rascalities of the world, and in this living score, the gallows is cheated of its own.*

Finally, Faxon tossed down the gauntlet: "Prentiss wants our scalp: we propose a plan by which he may get that valuable article." The colonel could choose 150 of his best fighters "or 250 of his lager-bier Dutchmen." Faxon would find 100 Columbus worthies as challengers. "Then let both parties meet where there will be no interruption at the scalping business, and the longest pole will knock the persimmon," Faxon vowed. "If he does not accept this proposal, he is a coward."

Prentiss ignored Faxon, but Russell suspected that Prentiss was more wounded by the editor's poison pen than the colonel admitted.

In the fall of 1861, Faxon returned to Confederate service. He evidently survived the war but apparently did not return to Columbus.

The Great Graves County Gun Grab

The great Graves County gun grab didn't make the history books. "It's all but unknown," said Lon Carter Barton, a teacher and historian from Mayfield. "But it's quite a story."

The heist happened in 1861. A band of Paducah Rebels, in cahoots with a state legislator, swiped nine hundred state-owned muskets and six cannons from the Graves County seat.

The thieves made headlines in Memphis and Louisville newspapers. The crime outraged authorities in then neutral Kentucky. They demanded that the weapons be returned. Evidently none of them were.

The arms belonged to the State Guard, Kentucky's mostly pro-Southern militia.

To check the State Guard, the Unionist-majority General Assembly created the pro-Union Home Guard.

Colonel Lloyd Tilghman of Paducah commanded the State Guard in the Purchase. He was an outspoken secessionist and was at the Mayfield convention. Tilghman did not want his precious ordnance winding up in Home Guard hands. Neither did the colonel's friend, Confederate Captain Henry Clay King, who was also from Paducah.

King had recruited a company of Rebel cavalry in and around his hometown. "His men were known as the 'Hell Hounds,'" Barton said.

On July 13, 1861, King, based at the Confederate camp at Union City, led his men to Mayfield to seize the State Guard arms for the Southern side. Graves County Judge A.R. Boone, a Confederate sympathizer, was in charge of the arms cache, Barton said.

Boone, another Mayfield convention attendee, urged King to leave the guns alone. The judge told him that Kentucky was sure to secede, arguing that swiping the weapons would hurt the Confederate cause in the state. Thus, King led the Hell Hounds back to Union City empty-handed, according to Barton.

The captain changed his mind and set out for Mayfield again on July 16. Anxious not to violate the Bluegrass State's precarious neutrality, the Union City camp commander sent a force of Tennesseans to stop King and his men, the *Memphis Avalanche* noted.

Three days later, King and the Hell Hounds sneaked off to Mayfield and grabbed the guns. The Rebels loaded the loot onto a southbound freight train, the *Louisville Journal* reported.

State Representative W.D. Lannom met the train at Hickman, a Mississippi River port and the Fulton County seat. He helped himself to four hundred muskets for his pro-Southern constituents in Fulton and Hickman Counties. The train took five hundred muskets and the artillery to Union City, according to the *Journal*.

Confederate officials promised to give back the guns they got. Apparently, though, they kept the firepower. But lawmaker Lannom, a leader of the pro-secession minority in the Kentucky House, vowed to keep his share of the State Guard weapons. When state officials ordered him to surrender the weapons, he refused, old state records show.

Lannom said that the Fulton and Hickman countians who had the muskets would agree to become Home Guards. Otherwise, he doubted that they "would permit any removal of these arms from their vicinity."

State authorities knew that Fulton and Hickman Counties, like the rest of the Purchase, were Rebel to the core. They repeated their demand that the guns be given up and even filed suit to get them back, state records also reveal.

It was all for naught. In the summer of 1861, Tilghman led most of his State Guards into Confederate service. Apparently, they were equipped with most of the stolen muskets and cannons.

Lannom did not return to Frankfort. Instead of seeking reelection, he helped raise the Seventh Kentucky Confederate Infantry Regiment in the fall of 1861. He was named lieutenant colonel of the all-Purchase outfit. His men may have been armed with his cut of the state weapons. Lannom survived the war. Promoted to general, Tilghman died in battle.

Meanwhile, Boone was elected to the General Assembly as a secessionist in August 1861. The House expelled Boone as a traitor after he helped organize the bogus Confederate government for the Bluegrass State.

Nonetheless, Boone proved that treason can pay, at least in western Kentucky. "He was elected to Congress after the Civil War," Barton said. A Democrat, Boone served from 1875 to 1879.

"The Blood of Boone"

The biggest Civil War recruiting camp for Kentucky Confederates was in Tennessee.

"Camp Boone" reads a state historical marker next to U.S. Highway 79 near Clarksville. Nothing but the sign commemorates where Kentucky's famous "Orphan Brigade" joined the Rebel army. "It was just farmland then and probably hasn't changed much since the Civil War," said Nicky Hughes, curator of historic sites for the city of Frankfort, Kentucky's capital.

The highway marker is located about two miles south of the Kentucky border. Camp Boone—named for Daniel Boone, the Bluegrass State's great pioneer hero—long ago returned to farmland. "But the spring where the soldiers got their water is still there," said Hughes, also a historian and writer who once portrayed a Rebel recruit in a living history program at the old campsite.

Kentucky was officially neutral when the camp opened in July 1861. "It was almost literally a stone's throw from the state line," said Hughes, who also reenacted the Civil War in Yankee blue. "It was pretty easy to get to."

Camp Boone was started by Colonel "Temp" Withers, Robert A. Johnson and James W. Hewitt, all secessionists from mostly pro-Union Louisville. Other Louisville citizens of Rebel sentiment chipped in money for the camp.

Ed Porter Thompson's 1898 *History of the Orphan Brigade* notes that Camp Boone was "two miles to the right of the Louisville and Memphis railroad, and seven miles from Clarksville, in a heavily-timbered forest, well supplied with water." The author, a brigade veteran, added that "fields furnishing sufficient open space for drilling large commands were convenient."

Rebel brass sought volunteers from across the Bluegrass State. Many came. Most of them were mustered into the "Orphan Brigade," an infantry outfit that fought in almost every big battle in the western theatre of America's bloodiest war. The Confederate soldiers earned their nickname after Kentucky stayed in the Union. Thus, they became Rebel "orphans" of a Yankee state.

"Unable, like Tennessee or Mississippi or Alabama soldiers, to see their homeland, and, with fortune, visit their firesides, the Kentuckians were outcasts, fighting for a cause their state denied," wrote William C. Davis in *The Orphan Brigade: The Kentucky Confederates Who Couldn't Go Home.* "They were orphans of the storm."

"I Search, and Can Not Find…Any Declaration, or Intimation, that You Entertain Any Desire for the Preservation of the Federal Union"

Imagine the U.S. Army opening a base in Kentucky and the governor telling the president to close it.

Early in the Civil War, the Yankees established Camp Dick Robinson near Bryantsville in Garrard County. It was the first Union recruiting center south of the Ohio River.

Beriah Magoffin, governor of then neutral Kentucky, sent a letter to President Abraham Lincoln demanding that he disband the post. Lincoln refused.

The Union-leaning General Assembly would not shut the camp either, said James C. Klotter, Kentucky state historian. "That would not be the only time in Kentucky's history when the governor and the legislature disagreed," added Klotter, who is also an author and history professor at Georgetown College.

A state historical marker on U.S. 27 near the Kentucky Highway 34 junction notes that Lincoln authorized Nelson, with whom he had met

Left: Governor Beriah Magoffin. *Courtesy of the Kentucky Historical Society.*

Below: Dick Robinson's farmhouse. *Photo by the author.*

about arming the Home Guard, to start the Yankee base. Garrard County was staunchly pro-Union.

Camp Dick Robinson was "named for Richard M. Robinson, a Union supporter, who offered house and farm as campsite," according to the marker. "Noted stagecoach stop, the house was also Nelson's headquarters." The dwelling still stands, but nothing is left of the camp.

The first recruits arrived at Camp Dick Robinson in August 1861, shortly after elections enhanced the Unionist majority in the legislature. Pro-Union refugees from eastern Tennessee also enlisted at the camp. "The Confederates tried to use the base's presence in the state as a wedge to drive Kentucky into Southern ranks, but to no avail," Klotter said.

Magoffin, who sympathized with the South, got nowhere with Lincoln either. "It is with regret I search, and can not find, in your not very short letter, any declaration, or intimation, that you entertain any desire for the preservation of the Federal Union," E. Merton Coulter quoted the president's reply.

Kentucky officially sided with the Union in September 1861, after Rebel and then Yankee armies invaded the western part of the state. Later, Camp Dick Robinson was replaced by Camp Nelson, named for William O. Nelson, in Jessamine County.

Klotter suspects that most of the soldiers who trained at Camp Dick Robinson remembered the post "not because its presence strengthened their cause, but rather because there they first came together in the army. There many drilled for the first time, first ate army rations, first became soldiers."

Men perished at Camp Dick Robinson, but not from enemy bullets. A measles epidemic killed several recruits. "For the survivors, the camp would be a grim reminder of what war soon would be like for all—a time of death and dying," Klotter said.

REBEL PIRATES HELPED MAKE KENTUCKY A YANKEE STATE

Pirates were more than a bane on the bounding main. Paducah-based brigands helped nudge neutral Kentucky into the Civil War. They also got the city sued, said Paducah historian and author John Robertson. "The city lost and had to pay $30,000 in damages, too," he added.

The USS *Lexington*, right, at Shiloh. *Courtesy of the Library of Congress.*

The steamboat *W.B. Terry* terrorized the Tennessee River in the summer of 1861, according to the *Louisville Journal*. Instead of flying the Jolly Roger, the *Terry* sported a Confederate flag.

On August 10, 1861, the *Terry*'s evidently well-armed crew pirated a load of tobacco from the Louisville steamer *Pocahontas* at Pine Bluff, in Calloway County. The brigands sold their booty in Rebel Tennessee, according to the disapproving *Journal*.

Twelve days later, the *Terry* was back in Paducah, where the Ohio and Tennessee Rivers join. The steamer reputedly was filled with contraband for the Confederates.

Suddenly, the USS *Lexington*, a Yankee gunboat, chugged into the harbor from Cairo. The *Terry*'s crew, "evidently suspecting my object, left the boat hastily," according to a report by Captain R.N. Stembel of the *Lexington* that was quoted in *The Official Records of the War of the Rebellion*.

His bluejackets grabbed the *Terry* without bloodshed. The Yankee sailors lashed the little steamer to the *Lexington* and towed the prize back to Cairo. Incensed, the *Terry*'s crew, led by the boat's captain, soon evened the score.

Helped by a mob, they commandeered the Evansville mail boat, *Samuel Orr*, and ran it up the Tennessee River to the Rebels. According to the *Official Records*, Captain W.H. McClurg of the *Orr* and others claimed that the "assailants" included "Captain Johnson, late commander of the steamboat W.B. Terry, White Fowler, A.M. Winston, and about 40 or 50 other persons, we believe all citizens of Paducah." He claimed that the mob fired several shots, "wounding two persons."

Union General John C. Fremont in St. Louis heard about the *Terry-Orr* tit for tat and advised Washington that "events have thus transpired clearly indicating the complicity of citizens of Kentucky with the Rebel forces, and showing the impractibility of carrying on operations in that direction without involving the Kentucky shore."

Confederate troops seized Hickman and Columbus, both on the Mississippi, September 3. General Ulysses S. Grant and a Yankee army captured Paducah on September 6. Soon afterward, Kentucky officially declared for the Union, but Paducah chafed under Yankee occupation for the rest of the war.

The *Terry* ended up "as a transport in support of the Western Gunboat flotilla," according to the U.S. Army Transportation Museum at Fort Eustis, Virginia. "An early combat loss on the Tennessee River, she was captured and burned by Confederate forces."

The *Orr* became part of the Confederate navy, though only briefly. As Union forces swept up the Tennessee in early 1862, the Rebels torched several boats, including the *Orr*, to prevent their capture.

When the Paducah men seized the *Samuel Orr*, McClurg valued his loss at about $25,000—$15,000 for the boat, which he said was new, and approximately $10,000 for the cargo, according to the *Official Records*. He also admitted that "some of the leading citizens of the town were loud in their condemnations of this act" but added that "no measures were taken, as far as we know, to prevent it."

Thus in 1867, two years after the war ended, McClurg and others sued the City of Paducah in federal court over the *Orr's* loss. "They were awarded a total of $30,000 in damages," Robertson said.

"I NEVER AFTER SAW SUCH CONSTERNATION DEPICTED ON THE FACES OF THE PEOPLE"

Ulysses S. Grant's road to military glory began in Paducah, the first town he captured in the Civil War.

Grant's Yankees were mostly unwelcome in Paducah. "I never after saw such consternation depicted on the faces of the people," the general wrote in *Personal Memoirs of U.S. Grant*. "Men, women and children came

General Ulysses S. Grant. *Courtesy of the Kentucky Historical Society.*

out of their doors looking pale and frightened at the presence of the invader. They were expecting rebel troops that day."

Dutifully, he issued an official occupation proclamation, promising Paducah residents that he had arrived to defend them against the Rebels. "This was evidently a relief to them," Grant wrote. "But the majority would have preferred the presence of the other army."

Most citizens of Hickman and Columbus were glad to see the Rebels. In his proclamation, Grant promised to protect Paducah from the Confederate "enemy." A reporter for the *St. Louis Republican* observed that the townsfolk "did not appear to appreciate the favor."

One of Grant's men, an Illinois sergeant, did not seem to mind the less-than-warm reception, according to *The Life of Billy Yank: The Common Soldier of the Union* by Bell Irvin Wiley. He quoted an Illinois sergeant's letter to his family: "I fell in love with Paducah while I was there…They hollered 'Hurrah for Jeff [Davis]'…but that's all right. I could write until tomorrow morning about Paducah."

CAMPUS LOVER'S LANE IS A CIVIL WAR TRENCH

The old pathway that furrows the rocky top of College Heights is a well-known campus landmark at Western Kentucky University in Bowling Green, the Warren County seat.

Some students know it as a lover's lane. It was meant for war.

"It's part of a Civil War trench," said Lowell H. Harrison, a historian and author who taught at Western for many years. "The *College Heights Herald*, the student newspaper, will feature an article about it every few years or so. But I doubt a lot of students know that the path dates from the Civil War."

This Civil War trench is a campus walkway at Western Kentucky University. *Photo by the author.*

General Albert Sidney Johnston. *Courtesy of the Kentucky Historical Society.*

The path follows the bottom of a stone-walled trench that Confederate troops dug when they occupied Bowling Green in the fall of 1861. The town straddled the Rebels' Kentucky defense line, which stretched eastward to Cumberland Gap and westward to Columbus.

"The Confederates fortified most high points in Bowling Green, including College Heights," Harrison said. "The fort here was one of the smaller ones."

Even so, it was strategically sited. The Louisville & Nashville Railroad ran by on one side. A highway between the two cities was on the other.

About seventy-five yards long and spanned by a little concrete bridge, the campus walkway is the best preserved of Bowling Green's Civil War fortifications, according to Harrison.

"The path is also one of only about two places on campus where you can walk with your date and be alone," said Barry Rose, a *Chattanooga Times Free Press* copy editor and a former *College Heights Herald* reporter.

After Grant captured Forts Henry and Donelson in Tennessee in February 1862, the Confederates abandoned their Kentucky defense line, including Bowling Green, which was the Rebel "capital" of the Bluegrass State. Yankee troops took the town.

The blue-clad soldiers named the strongpoint on College Heights (Vinegar Hill in the Civil War) Fort Lytle, but in the 1920s, some at Western decided that the fort needed a Confederate name. (Never mind that Bowling Green was mainly pro-Union.)

Western officials started calling the strongpoint Fort Albert Sidney Johnston. He was a Kentucky-born general who had been commander of the Confederate forces in the Bluegrass State. He was killed at the Battle of Shiloh in April 1862.

"If the Confederates actually named [the fort]…we don't know what the name was," said Harrison. His campus office was a short walk from the path.

Union troops bolstered the Rebel defense works. "Bowling Green was so strongly fortified that the Confederates didn't try to take it any time during the war," Harrison said. Indeed, when General Braxton Bragg invaded Kentucky in the autumn of 1862, he gave Bowling Green a wide berth, said Harrison, who wrote *The Civil War in Kentucky* and other books.

Rebel Vowed Never to Shave until the Yankees Were Whipped

Elisha B. Kirtley "had many 'close shaves'" in the Civil War, but not a whisker was clipped.

Before the Paradise resident joined the Rebel army in September 1861, he promised that "he would not shave again until the Confederate government was established beyond all doubt," according to *A History of Muhlenberg County* by Otto A. Rothert.

Kirtley ended up permanently retiring his razor.

Kirtley lived for more than a half-century after the Civil War ended in 1865, Rothert wrote. The old Rebel seems to be all but forgotten in Paradise, his Muhlenberg County hometown.

"I'd say the story of Elisha Kirtley is not that well known anywhere in the county," said Bobby Anderson, a local historian, author and journalist from Beechmont. "But you can bet your boots if it's in Rothert, it's true."

A New History of Kentucky notes that Kirtley stuck to his pledge. He "died… still unshaven," the authors wrote.

Kirtleys still live in and around Muhlenberg County. Rodney Kirtley is a former Muhlenberg judge-executive. "As far as I know [Elisha Kirtley]…is not a close relative but he must have had a lot of faith in the Confederacy," he said.

Muhlenberg County was mostly pro-Union in the Civil War. But Elisha Kirtley opted for Rebel gray.

"On the 'fourth Sunday in September, 1861,'…[Kirtley] made preparations to join the Southern army," Rothert wrote. While he was shaving, he made his vow to "those who were in his room."

Kirtley walked to Bowling Green and enlisted in the First Kentucky Confederate Cavalry Regiment. Later, he switched to the Ninth Kentucky Infantry Regiment.

"At any rate, although he had many 'close shaves' at Shiloh, Chickamauga, and Missionary Ridge, he never shaved his face after the 'fourth Sunday in September, 1861,' but wore a long beard during the remainder of his life, more than fifty years," Rothert wrote. "Resolutions of similar nature were often made by Federal as well as Confederate soldiers, and many of them were carried out."

Lyon County Church Still Holed by a Yankee Bullet

When the old Saratoga Springs United Methodist Church in Lyon County was spruced up with new siding, the congregation took care to preserve a bullet hole.

It is framed and under glass. "A Yankee Minié ball struck the side of the church, and the hole has been there ever since," said Sam Steger, an author and historian from nearby Princeton, the Caldwell County seat.

About 300 Union soldiers got the best of 160 or so Confederates in the half-hour fight at the church in deep western Kentucky. The date was October 26, 1861.

"Several communities claim to have been where the first shot was fired in Kentucky during the war," Steger said. "But one of the first encounters between Blue and Gray was at Saratoga Springs."

The little white frame house of worship on Kentucky Highway 293 South was two years old when America's bloodiest war arrived on its doorstep. Captain M.D. Wilcox's company of Confederate cavalry was scouting in the neighborhood and using the Saratoga church as a base.

"The men were from Lyon and adjacent Caldwell counties," Steger said. "They were part of the First Kentucky Cavalry, a regiment commanded by Colonel Benjamin Hardin Helm, whose wife was Mary Todd Lincoln's half-sister."

Three companies from the Ninth Illinois Infantry surprised Wilcox and his troopers, killing six and wounding several more, including one fatally. According to the Union commander, the rest of the Confederates "fled in every direction—some on foot, others on horseback," Steger said.

The attacking Yankees also helped themselves to abandoned Confederate horses, saddles, other gear and weapons. In addition, they arrested C.F. Jenkins, who was described as a "notorious secessionist," according to Steger.

Yankee casualties were just three men wounded; Caldwell countian Elbert Beck may have shot all three himself, Steger said. "Supposedly, he ran out on the porch of the church, fired both barrels of his double-barreled shotgun and hit a captain, a corporal and another man," Steger said. "Presumably, he then escaped."

Except for the bullet hole in an old white clapboard, there is nothing to commemorate the skirmish at the Saratoga church, which may have

Right: Civil War bullet hole in Saratoga Springs Church. *Photo by the author.*

Below: Saratoga Springs Church. *Photo by the author.*

sheltered wounded soldiers after the shooting stopped. Supposedly, the floorboards are still bloodstained.

Its battle scar aside, the Saratoga church is historic in its own right. It was built in 1859, replacing a log meetinghouse that dated to 1822.

"KENTUCKY'S FIRST BLOOD IN THE WAR OF THE REBELLION"

Some say the fiery ghost of Yankee Private Granville Allen still haunts the Big Hill, where he supposedly became the first Kentucky soldier killed in the Civil War.

The haunted hill is located near Morgantown, the Butler County seat.

Purportedly, the poltergeist appears as a flash of light or a fireball at night. Skeptics suggest that the phenomenon is nothing more than methane gas escaping from old Butler County coal pits.

A rectangular, lichen-dappled sandstone tablet set in a rock outcropping close to the old roadway where he died in 1861 commemorates the shedding of Kentucky's "First Blood in the War of the Rebellion."

Was Allen the first of thousands of Kentuckians to die in America's bloodiest conflict? A metal state historical society marker on Kentucky Highway 403 near the monument notes only that he was the "first Union soldier killed in west Kentucky."

The date is also disputed. The marker notes that he died skirmishing Rebels on October 29, 1861. The memorial stone displays it as October 27.

"First Union soldier killed in west Kentucky" might be right. After all, Steger said that Rebels died at the Saratoga Springs skirmish on October 26.

Nonetheless, Allen's army tenure was short. The marker explains that Colonel John H. McHenry enrolled him at Calhoun, seat of neighboring Ohio County, on October 3, 1861. McHenry commanded the Seventeenth Kentucky.

In addition to Saratoga Springs and the Big Hill, other places in Kentucky have been cited as the place where the first Bluegrass State soldier was slain in the Civil War. So the actual spot where the first death occurred will probably never be known.

Anyway, in 1894, the Granville Allen Post of the Grand Army of the Republic, a local branch of the national Union veterans' organization,

The Granville Allen Monument. *Photo by the author.*

had the stone tablet placed beside the road that crossed the Big Hill. After Highway 403 was built, the old road was abandoned.

NATION'S OLDEST CIVIL WAR MONUMENT UNDERGOING RESTORATION IN LOUISVILLE

The epitaph has worn off America's oldest Civil War monument.

"Here rest the first martyrs of the Thirty-second, the first German regiment of Indiana," Private August Bloedner, a stonemason, chiseled into the slab of gray Green River limestone after the small but bloody Battle of Rowletts Station near Munfordville, the Hart County seat. "They were fighting nobly in defense of the free Constitution of the United States of America."

Bloedner's tribute was in German.

In 1867, the government moved the memorial and the remains of fourteen of Bloedner's fallen comrades from Munfordville to the national cemetery within historic Cave Hill Cemetery in Louisville. Eventually, the monument

The Bloedner Monument. *Courtesy of Conservation Solutions, Inc. & the National Cemetery Administration, United States Department of Veterans Affairs.*

began to crumble. Fearing that it might not last, cemetery officials had it shipped to the University of Louisville for restoration.

The monument will not return, according to John Trowbridge, command historian of the Kentucky National Guard. "We need to get it indoors out of the weather," he said. "We are meeting to determine the best location to showcase the monument."

Trowbridge and others had hoped to save the monument where it stood in the cemetery. They had a makeshift wooden shelter built over the stonework, covering it almost to the bottom.

"Cave Hill is a popular tourist attraction," Trowbridge said. "So we put up a plaque next to the monument explaining what it is." A sign explains that the monument was removed in December 2008.

Fought on December 17, 1861, the Battle of Rowletts Station was one of the first battles in Kentucky. About 130 men were killed or wounded on both sides.

Outnumbered six to one, a half-dozen companies of the Thirty-second Indiana Infantry, a German immigrant regiment, whipped the Rebels, most of them from Arkansas and Texas. "One regiment of Texas Rangers [cavalry], two regiments of infantry, and six pieces of rebel artillery, in all over three thousand men, were defeated by five hundred German soldiers," Bloedner proudly put in the epitaph.

When the Confederates attacked, the Hoosiers were protecting a pontoon bridge they had built over the Green River. Their ranks included Bloedner, who was from Cincinnati, and a few volunteers from Louisville.

The Battle of Rowletts Station was the Thirty-second Indiana's baptism of fire. But the green troops fought like veterans, according to Trowbridge. "Basically, the regiment went into the old box formation and held the Confederates off," he said.

After the Rebels retreated, the Thirty-second Indiana guarded the bridge for about a month. That gave Bloedner time to sculpt the memorial.

"He took a large piece of limestone from near the Green River and expertly carved onto it an account of the battle in German," Trowbridge said. "He included the names, places and dates of birth of the men killed. He surmounted the monument with a recess into which he carved patriotic symbols, including an eagle clutching a brace of cannons flanked by American flags."

The dead from the Thirty-second Indiana were buried on a hilltop in Munfordville not far from the battlefield. "The memorial was placed flat on the ground to mark the graves, sometime in January 1862," Trowbridge said.

Bloedner survived the war, apparently fighting with his regiment at Shiloh, Stone's River, Chickamauga, Chattanooga and in the Atlanta campaign. It is unknown if he attended a ceremony welcoming his monument to Cave Hill, where it was placed upright.

Several Louisville citizens, most of them German-born or of German ancestry, contributed money for a Bedford, Indiana limestone base for the monument, Trowbridge said. "In memory of the First Victims of the 32. Reg. Indiana Vol. Who fell at the Battle of Rowlettd [sic] Station Dec.17, 1861" reads its English inscription.

"SHE JUST ABOUT STARTED THE CIVIL WAR AROUND HERE ALL BY HERSELF"

A teenage Confederate heroine is buried at an old Sacramento cemetery within rifle range of where she helped General Nathan Bedford Forrest win his first Civil War battle.

Two tombstones mark Molly Morehead Stowers's grave. Neither reveals that the eighteen-year-old woman risked her life to warn Forrest that Yankees were in Sacramento, her little McLean County hometown. Nor do the memorials say that Forrest cited her for "infusing nerve into my arms and kindling knightly chivalry within my heart."

Forrest, one of the Confederacy's most famous cavalry commanders, did not mention Morehead by name in his official report of the Sacramento battle. But she was identified as "a Miss Morehead" in *The Campaigns of Lieut.-Gen. N.B. Forrest, and of Forrest's Cavalry*, a book written by General Thomas Jordan and J.P. Pryor and published in 1868.

Allen Taylor Nall said that "she just about started the Civil War around here all by herself. She was rarin' to go."

Blue and gray forces collided at Sacramento on December 28, 1861. "Molly was out riding horses with her sister, Sarah, that day," said Nall, from Calhoun. "When Molly saw the Yankees, she told Sarah to go home. Molly rode off to find Forrest."

According to Jordan and Pryor, Morehead was "obliged to pass through the Federal column" to tell Forrest about the Union troops. When she reached the Rebels, they beheld "a beautiful girl…her features glowing with excitement, her fallen tresses swayed by the air," Jordan and Pryor wrote.

An olive-green metal state historical marker at the junction of Kentucky Highways 81 and 181 more or less marks the spot where Morehead tipped off the Confederates. The plaque doesn't mention her.

Morehead had crossed paths with a small cavalry patrol returning to camp at Calhoun, where ten thousand Union troops guarded Lock and Dam No. 2 on the Green River. The patrol was looking for Forrest and his three hundred gray-clad cavalrymen who were believed to be in the area.

While most McLean countians were pro-Union, Morehead's father, Hugh Morehead, was a Southern sympathizer. Reportedly, Forrest visited the family while scouting the area himself. It is unknown how Molly knew where Forrest was.

Apparently, Morehead was spoiling for a fight with the Yankees herself. She rode south from Sacramento toward Greenville, hoping to find the Rebel cavalry.

Jordan and Pryor wrote that "waving her hat in the air," Morehead "urged the Confederates to 'hurry up;' and she rode back [toward Sacramento] at a gallop for several hundred yards by the side of…Forrest." The authors added, "Such was the spirit which animated so many of the Southern women."

Fearing for the teen's safety, Forrest ordered her to leave before the shooting started. But thanks to Morehead, Forrest was able to attack the outnumbered Yankees and force them to flee before reinforcements could arrive from Calhoun. The Rebels lost only two men in the brief fight; Union casualties were eleven dead and forty missing.

Molly, whose real name was Mary Susan Morehead, survived the war and married Dr. George Stowers, a dentist, in 1866. She died in 1870 while giving birth to their infant son, who also perished with her. Mother and child were buried together in the Cumberland Presbyterian Church Cemetery in Sacramento.

Weather-beaten and dappled with gray lichen, her old white marble tombstone is silent about her Southern service in the Battle of Sacramento. A newer gray granite tombstone, placed about 1970 according to Nall, doesn't mention it either.

Her story was included in a pamphlet that maps out a "Battle of Sacramento Driving Tour." Molly Morehead Stowers's final resting place is tour stop number seven.

"THE PRIDE OF THE ARMY, AND THE TERROR OF THE GUNBOATS"

It was enough to make a preacher cuss.

Supposedly, careless soldiers had let a shell jam "Lady Polk," the 7.5-ton long-range gun that the Confederates at Columbus used to drive the Yankees away from Belmont, Missouri, across the Mississippi.

Their general, Leonidas Polk, an ex-Episcopal bishop, was furious that the big gun named for his wife was out of commission. He reputedly ordered the cannon crew to fire the gun to clear it.

The artillerymen knew that Lady Polk would blow up and probably kill them all. The gun did burst, claiming the lives of nine men and tearing Polk's clothes off, or so the story went.

It was also said that a young Rebel put on a fresh new uniform so he would look nice for his funeral. "It's a well-known story all right," said John Kelly Ross Jr., a local historian. "There's even a cannon fragment, supposedly from 'Lady Polk,' mounted on a pedestal at Columbus-Belmont State Park."

Ross, who has spent years researching the Civil War in Columbus, believes that the story is not true. He says the explosion was an accident. Polk got a bum rap, Ross insists, adding that the jagged chunk of iron at the park might even be from a different cannon.

Nonetheless, newspapers and some Rebel officers charged that Polk ignored warnings that the cannon would explode. A 1904 *Confederate Veteran* magazine article blamed the general for the disaster.

Lady Polk fired ten-inch-diameter shells. The iron-barreled gun dwarfed all the other big guns at cannon-bristling Columbus, according to Ross, who lives in Clinton, the seat of Hickman County.

Ross, curator at the Hickman County Museum in Clinton, said that the Rebels nicknamed some of their other cannons. "There was 'Soul Searcher,' 'Snorter,' 'Yankee Smolluxer,' 'Rib Smasher' and 'Cunning Cuss,'" he said.

The Confederates aimed their cannons at Belmont on November 7, 1861, when Grant and his army seized the outpost. They had to fight their

Cannon fragment at Columbus-Belmont State Park. *Photo by the author.*

36

way out after the Rebels crossed over from heavily fortified Columbus and surrounded them.

Polk's hometown newspaper, the *New Orleans Times Picayune*, reported that Lady Polk was "the pride of the army, and the terror of the gunboats." It proved to be frightening to the Rebels.

Following the Battle of Belmont, the gun's crew reportedly forgot to unload the ordnance. When the barrel cooled, it shrank down tightly on an unfired shell. Despite the danger of an explosion, Polk allegedly ordered the gun discharged.

"After the 1904 *Confederate Veteran* story came out, several Confederate officers, including two men standing beside Polk when the cannon exploded, wrote in to correct the story," Ross said. "They said the battery commander just wanted to impress Polk by aiming the gun upriver and showing him how far 'Lady Polk' would fire."

Polk narrowly escaped death in the blast. Reputedly, he was dazed.

Ross said that the story of Polk as a callous commander was told for years in Columbus, even at the state park. He decided to try again to clear Polk's name, writing an article defending the general that was published in a 1990 issue of *Confederate Veteran*.

In another article, printed in the *Hickman County Gazette*, Ross claimed that the cannon fragment in the park is not part of Lady Polk. "It is from a smaller, 32-pounder gun," Ross said "It's impossible to say where it came from, though."

Ross said that when Union troops occupied Columbus in early 1862, they shipped the fragments of Lady Polk to the U.S. Navy Yard at nearby Mound City, Illinois.

"After the war, they made an arm chair out of the pieces and put it in a locust grove inside the navy yard," Ross said. The naval facility and the chair are long gone.

"Pot Pye" for Christmas Dinner

William Jackson Perren of the Forty-first Illinois Infantry promised a special holiday meal for Confederates aiming to spend Christmas in Union-occupied Smithland, the Livingston County seat.

"We will set at the head of the table and wate on them with pot pye cokt in a stove knone by the name of the columby pop gun," the Kentuckian wrote his parents two days before Yuletide 1861.

Translation: The Yankees would shoot the Rebels with their mighty Columbiad cannon.

Randa Ramsey of Gracey treasures her great-great-uncle's letter, which he penned to R.G. and Marey Perren. "Remane your son til Deth," Perren concluded.

Private Perren perished on the first day of the Battle of Shiloh, April 6, 1862. He was twenty-one years old.

Perren was from Dycusburg, in nearby Crittenden County, where his family also lived. Apparently, he joined Company I of the Forty-first Illinois after it arrived in Smithland, where the Cumberland River joins the Ohio. Following his capture of Paducah, Grant sent some of his troops to seize Smithland. Union troops fortified both strategic towns against the Confederates.

Perren was one of several Yankee volunteers from mostly pro-Union Crittenden County. "You can see from the letter that my great-great-uncle spelled words like they sounded to him," Ramsey said.

Perren added, "The cesesh ["secesh," short for "secessionists"] say that they are agone to take din[n]er in our fort a[t] Christmas." The enemy didn't show up.

Nonetheless, Union forces braced themselves for battle. They erected a pair of stout-walled earthworks on high ground overlooking Smithland and the rivers. The bastions were known collectively as Fort Smith.

The larger strongpoint, which was razed long ago, included the Columbiad, which fired sixty-four-pound shells, and a thirty-two-pounder cannon. The smaller work, which survives on a wooded hilltop above Livingston Central High School, sheltered another thirty-two-pounder.

In his letter, Perren assured his loved ones that he was "doing well [and] hoping that theze few lines may find you all injoying the same blessing[.]" He invited his father "to come down and see our fort and our Company and bring of few of the boys with you." All "will find good friends and warm h[e]arts among the solgers…[who are]…polite and cind," he said.

Perren left a wife, Martha Ann Perren, when he signed up for the army. "She had one son by a previous marriage, and they had a son together," Ramsey said.

The soldier hoped that R.G. Perren might look after Martha Ann and the children. "Now Father do not forget to keep Marthey an in wood and I will try to send one rebel home when they come to take din[n]er with us," he wrote.

He also asked his father to "go to James Rupp and get 4 dollers that he oze me and give it to Marthey an[.]" Perren added, "I wont you to go and marke my hogs if you pleze[.] I am a feard that they will stray of[f] and get lost before I can at[t]end to it."

Perren did not stay long in Smithland. In February 1862, the Forty-first Illinois helped Grant's army capture Fort Donelson, farther up the Cumberland River at Dover, Tennessee.

Less than two months later, Grant defeated another Rebel army at the Battle of Shiloh, Tennessee, near the Tennessee River. Perren lost his life the first day of the savage two-day fight. "We think he was buried at Shiloh," Ramsey said.

Perren is not listed among the named burials at Shiloh National Cemetery, which is inside Shiloh National Military Park. But several graves contain the remains of unknown soldiers.

Ramsey said that her family doesn't know what became of Martha Ann and the boys. "Supposedly, she was from Illinois and may have gone back there with them."

"The Day the War Stopped in Kentucky"

The burial of Sister Mary Lucy Dosh was "the day the war stopped in Kentucky," says Paducah historian Penny Baucum Fields. America's bloodiest conflict halted long enough in late 1861 for six Yankees and six Rebels to escort Sister Mary Lucy, twenty-two, to her grave.

The young nurse's story is all but forgotten, but an exhibit at Paducah's Market House Museum commemorates Sister Mary Lucy, who lost her life helping to save others. "I've seen guys cry when they read the story," said Fields, museum executive director. "The tragic death of a young nun inspires soldiers at war to put aside their differences, if just for a little while. It's quite a story."

Sister Mary Lucy succumbed to typhoid fever while nursing Union troops and Confederate prisoners of war. "She was held in such grateful esteem and affection that her body, escorted by an officer and a detail of soldiers, was taken to the U.S. Gunboat *Peacock* on a caisson, put aboard and transported to Uniontown, Kentucky, where it was carried to St. Vincent's Academy in Union County," wrote John T. Donovan in his 1934 book *The Catholic Church in Paducah, Kentucky*.

Sister Mary Lucy was born Barbara Dosh in Pennsylvania. "She and her sister were orphans who were taken in by the Sisters of Nazareth of Louisville," Fields said. Barbara had a talent for singing, so the nuns sent her to study music at St. Vincent's near Waverly, in Union County. "A wealthy couple wanted to adopt her, but she so loved the Sisters of Nazareth that she became a nun and was known henceforth as Sister Mary Lucy," Fields added.

When the Civil War broke out in 1861, Sister Mary Lucy was teaching music at St. Mary's Academy in Paducah. After Northern troops occupied the city, they appealed to the sisters at St. Mary's to help nurse the sick and wounded.

Although they were teachers, the nuns from St. Mary's, now St. Mary High School, did double duty as nurses. "The Sisters served in all the hospitals which were soon filled with cases of typhoid and other infectious diseases, and later with sick and wounded from the battlefields," Donovan wrote.

Some patients were captured Confederates, Fields said. "The nuns treated all of the patients the same," she added. "It was said that Sister Mary Lucy had a beautiful voice and sometimes sang softly as she worked." Sister Mary Lucy also ate less food so the patients could have more, according to Fields. "This apparently weakened her system, and she came down with typhoid fever." Sister Mary Lucy died on December 29, 1861.

"Even battle-hardened soldiers were heartbroken at the death of this selfless young nun," Fields said. "She had never raised a hand against anybody, and here she was struck down by this horrible disease."

Union authorities arranged a military funeral. Her honor guard was composed of a dozen officers, six in blue and six in gray. All were patients of Sister Mary Lucy. Her coffin was placed aboard the *Peacock*, the cannon-bristling gunboat draped in black.

The warship transported Sister Mary Lucy's remains up the Ohio River to Uniontown, where a wagon waited to take the coffin to the little cemetery at St. Vincent's Academy. "The soldiers were convalescent at best," Fields said. "In their weakened state, they risked catching pneumonia in the cold out on the river."

It was dark when the *Peacock* reached Uniontown. "They put torches on the wagon, and the funeral procession traveled another seven miles down a dirt road to the cemetery," Fields said. After a brief funeral service, her body was laid to rest. "Before they left, the officers, with the permission of the church, gave her a military salute."

THE CONFEDERACY'S "VALLEY FORGE"

Camp Beauregard doesn't rate more than a few lines in history books. But Lon Carter Barton likened the local Rebel outpost to Valley Forge.

"If there was a Confederate Valley Forge, this was it," he said. "The suffering was terrible in the cold, rain, sleet and snow."

Occupied by about 5,000 Rebels from a half-dozen states early in the Civil War, the camp crowned a high hill near Water Valley in south Graves County. As many as 1,400 Southerners died at Camp Beauregard, but they didn't fall to Yankee bullets. Disease claimed their lives in 1861–62.

A gray stone monument commemorates the old Confederate camp, now a cemetery at which people are still buried. Rowed up, soldierlike, are sixteen military tombstones that mark the graves of Mississippi and Missouri Rebels. But most of the Confederate dead were buried in mass graves. They are unidentified.

The Camp Beauregard Monument. *Photo by the author.*

The camp was named for General Pierre G.T. Beauregard of Louisiana. A Southern hero, he had directed the bombardment of Fort Sumter, South Carolina, which started the Civil War. Beauregard was never at the camp, which the Confederates opened after they seized Hickman and Columbus.

While Camp Beauregard's fortifications were skimpy, it was well sited for defense, wrote Paducah journalist and historian Hall Allen in his 1961 book *Center of Conflict*. "It was located on a high hill surrounded by plains and open fields," he explained.

Barton said Camp Beauregard was located near plenty of water and firewood. Close, too, was a railroad that connected the camp to the Rebel post at Union City, about twenty miles away.

"By Christmas of 1861 upwards of 5,000 men were training on the hilltop," Allen wrote. "The troops were almost ready to take their places in the Southern battleline."

Even today, there is disagreement over what the deadly malady was at Camp Beauregard. "Some claim it was measles," Barton said. "Others say meningitis. It may have been both."

Part II

1862–1863

"Come Out Here, You Cowardly Rebels, and Show Your Gunboats"

Most Kentucky duels were fought with pistols. But it looked like honor would have to be settled warship to warship near Columbus early in the Civil War.

"Some people still saw war in terms of the old code duello," John Kelly Ross Jr. explained. He said the *New York Times* reported that Yankee Captain William D. "Dirty Bill" Porter challenged Rebel skipper Marsh J. Miller to "show yourself any morning in Prenty's [probably Puntney's] bend, and you shall meet with a traitor's fate."

The duel never came off, according to Ross. But Porter's challenge grabbed front-page headlines in the *Times*. "It must have been a slow news day," Ross said, chuckling.

Porter commanded the USS *Essex*, "the most powerful ironclad gunboat on the Mississippi River at the time," Ross said. Miller was captain of the *Grampus*, a little sternwheeler steamboat. "The *Grampus* was Porter's nemesis," Ross added.

The *Essex* was based near Cairo. The *Grampus* was from Columbus, about twelve miles down the Mississippi from Cairo. "The Union gunboats would test the defenses of Columbus," Ross said. "The *Grampus* would wait for them a few miles above Columbus, and blowing her steam

The USS *Essex. Courtesy of the Library of Congress.*

whistle, the little scout boat would race ahead of the Yankee fleet to warn the Confederates."

His vessel armed with only two or three small cannons, according to Ross, Miller prudently preferred flight to fight. Even so, the plodding *Essex* almost caught the speedy *Grampus* one time.

The Rebel boat was stopped upriver from Columbus so the crew could pick pawpaws, Ross said. "When they saw the Union fleet, the men rushed back to the boat and got away to Columbus."

Porter demanded a showdown. He sent the challenge to duel, possibly by truce boat, on January 18, 1862. "Come out here, you cowardly rebels, and show your gunboats," the *Times* quoted Porter.

Miller picked up the gauntlet. The *Times* published his reply: "SIR: The ironclad steamer GRAMPUS will meet the ESSEX at any point and any time your Honor might appoint, and show you that the power is in our hands."

The *Times* also printed Porter's reply to "the traitor Marsh Miller." "Dirty Bill" demanded, "If you desire to meet the ESSEX, show yourself any morning in Prenty's Bend, and you shall meet with a traitor's fate—if you have the courage to stand. God and our Country; 'Rebels offend both.'"

The *Essex* would have made kindling out of the *Grampus*, Ross said. "The *Essex* was a real ironclad. The *Grampus* wasn't. It was just a little wooden boat. But Porter was able to get a little cheap publicity out of the affair."

Miller kept the *Grampus* out of range of the *Essex*'s powerful cannons. The boat escaped with the Confederates when they abandoned Columbus in March 1862.

The *Grampus* served briefly as a scout boat at Island Number 10, a Rebel bastion near New Madrid, Missouri. But in April 1862 that strongpoint fell to the Yankees, too.

Miller's luck had run out. Cornered by the Union fleet, the captain ordered the crew to scuttle the *Grampus*.

Porter wasn't able to exact revenge. In February 1862, the *Essex* was badly damaged in Grant's seizure of Fort Henry on the Tennessee River, just below the Kentucky-Tennessee line. A Confederate cannonball sailed through an open gun port and exploded one of the *Essex*'s boilers. "It must have been a nightmare," Ross said. "Live steam killed fourteen men and burned twenty-eight more, including Porter. The war was no longer a game for 'Dirty Bill.'"

THE ZOLLIE TREE

A sapling sprouts from the remains of the old oak tree close to where Rebel General Felix K. Zollicoffer died in the Civil War Battle of Mill Springs in Pulaski County.

"It was called the 'Zollie Tree,' and it stood until it was blown down in a big storm in 1995," Gilbert Wilson said. "It was pretty rotten on the inside."

The tree was a mighty white oak, added Wilson, executive director of the Mill Springs Battlefield Association's museum. The nonprofit group also maintains the sixty-five-acre battleground near Nancy.

From 1902 until it toppled, the Zollie Tree was annually decorated with a memorial wreath in honor of the fallen general.

Zollicoffer's death was a case of mistaken identity. A cold rain was falling on January 19, 1862, when blue and gray armies collided at Mill Springs. Fog and battle smoke made it even harder to see.

Zollicoffer, a Tennessean, spied what he thought were Confederates shooting at other Confederates. He spurred his horse over to the soldiers and barked a cease-fire order.

He didn't know it was the Fourth Kentucky Infantry, Union, commanded by Colonel Speed S. Fry. "Or, when he got there, he did recognize it was the enemy and tried to bluff his way out by ordering a cease fire," Wilson said.

Zollicoffer was wearing a raincoat over his uniform. At that moment, two of Zollicoffer's aides appeared out of the fog. At least one of them, a lieutenant, recognized the soldiers as Union.

"He shouts, 'General, they are the enemy!' and shoots at Fry with his pistol," Wilson explained. The bluecoats quickly shot Zollicoffer and either killed outright or fatally wounded the aides.

General Felix K. Zollicoffer. *Courtesy of the Library of Congress.*

The name of the lieutenant who appeared from the fog was Henry M.R. Fogg.

Zollicoffer—supposedly shot by Fry himself—tumbled off his horse. "Some of the Confederates said they picked up his body and carried it about fifty feet but that it got so hot for them that they dropped it at the Zollie Tree," Wilson said. "The Union troops found it leaning up against the tree when they swept on by."

After they won the battle, the Yankees returned the remains of Zollicoffer and the two junior officers to the Rebels. Zollicoffer was buried in Nashville, where he lived, but not before Yankees helped themselves to souvenirs from the slain general.

"They pulled buttons off his uniform," Wilson said. "They cut off pieces of coat and even got some of his hair until a guard was put on his body to stop the souvenir hunting."

Union dead were buried individually at Mill Springs National Cemetery. Slain Confederates were interred in mass graves close to the Zollie Tree.

In 1902, Dorotha Burton, a ten-year-old girl who lived on the old battlefield, placed flowers on the Rebel graves. She wove blooms into an evergreen wreath and entwined it around the Zollie Tree.

Burton returned annually to decorate the old oak tree and the graves until 1947, when arthritis kept her from her self-appointed rounds. "Her family kept it up until the tree was destroyed in the storm," said Don Elmore, a former member of the association's board of directors.

The association salvaged what it could of the splintered Zollie Tree. The stump is in the museum. The rest was sawed up and crafted into pen and pencil sets and clocks. "We sell them and use the money to help us run the museum and preserve the battlefield," Wilson said.

From time to time, the association hosts bloodless reenactments of the Battle of Mill Springs, which claimed about 170 lives on both sides. Elmore is an ex-Confederate reenactor.

"We used to camp out around a Confederate burial site on the anniversary of the battle," he said. "One night we were standing around in our uniforms, leaning on our rifles, when this pickup truck stopped out in the road. The driver stared at us. He was drinking something out of a brown paper bag. We stared back. Then one of the guys who's got a great sense of humor said, 'All right, everybody back in the graves!' We all lay down. The guy in the truck took off. We figured the whiskey bottle hit the road about halfway up the hill. We'd also like to think he never drove and drank again."

"THEY ALL KNEW EACH OTHER BEFORE THE CIVIL WAR"

Rebel General Simon Bolivar Buckner surrendered Fort Donelson but not his Kentucky hospitality.

After he ran up the white flag, the Hart County native asked Yankee General Lew Wallace to breakfast. Twenty-three years later, Buckner agreed to serve as a pallbearer for General Ulysses S. Grant, to whom he relinquished Fort Donelson, a cannon-studded bastion that guarded the Cumberland against the Yankees.

"They all knew each other before the Civil War," said Jimmy Jobe, historian at Fort Donelson National Battlefield, near Dover, Tennessee. "Buckner and Grant, especially, were old friends. They were at West Point at the same time and fought together in the Mexican War."

Buckner, born near Munfordville, the Hart County seat, in 1823, helped Grant when he resigned from the army in 1854. Grant ended up in New York down on his luck and short of cash to pay for a hotel room. Grant contacted Buckner, who was also in the city. "Buckner agreed to guarantee the bill until Grant's father could send him the money," said Buzz Bazar, a retired Fort Donelson park ranger. "Grant didn't forget that."

Apparently, they didn't meet again until February 16, 1862, when Buckner gave up Fort Donelson to his old army buddy following a bloody three-day battle.

The earthen fort is well preserved in the national park. So are Confederate outer trenches and the wooden, two-story Dover Hotel, where Buckner officially capitulated to Grant.

Buckner recalled that after the surrender formalities Grant pulled him aside and offered him money. Buckner politely refused.

General Simon Bolivar Buckner. *Courtesy of the Kentucky Historical Society.*

General Lew Wallace. *Courtesy of the Library of Congress.*

Buckner was a captive at Fort Warren, Massachusetts. "Grant wrote Buckner a letter of introduction so he might be afforded better treatment when he got there," Bazar said. Released through a prisoner of war exchange, Buckner got back in Rebel gray. He fought in several more battles.

Before Grant arrived to accept Buckner's surrender, Wallace broke bread with the Kentuckian and his staff. Apparently, Wallace, from Indiana, also knew Buckner from the Mexican-American War of 1846–48.

"He met me with politeness and dignity," Wallace wrote in *Battles and Leaders of the Civil War*. "Turning to the officers at the table, he remarked: 'General Wallace, it is not necessary to introduce you to these gentlemen; you are acquainted with them all.'"

They rose and shook hands with Wallace. "I was then invited to breakfast, which consisted of corn bread and coffee, the best the gallant officer had in his kitchen," added Wallace, author of *Ben Hur: A Tale of the Christ*. "We sat at the table about an hour and a half."

Grant was elected president in 1868 and served two terms. Buckner was governor of Kentucky from 1887 to 1891.

In 1885, Buckner and his second wife, Delia, were honeymooning in Saratoga, New York. They decided to visit Grant, who was dying of throat cancer at nearby Mount McGregor.

Buckner tried to cheer Grant, who was unable to speak. He reminded the general of a badly wounded officer they knew from the Mexican-American War. Given up for dead, the man recovered. "There cannot be a cure in my case," Grant replied in a handwritten note. Grant died shortly after Buckner's visit and was entombed in New York City. Buckner was one of four pallbearers.

A *New York Times* reporter asked the ex-Rebel general how he felt about helping lay to rest the Yankees' greatest general. Buckner, according to the scribe, stiffly refused a response "except to say that General Grant had a great heart."

Buckner died in 1914. He was nearly ninety-one and the last surviving Confederate lieutenant general, according to the *Kentucky Encyclopedia*.

The Great Locomotive Chase

A courageous Kentuckian prompted the awarding of the first Medals of Honor in U.S. history.

James J. Andrews of Flemingsburg, the Fleming County seat, was a Civil War hero who gave his life for his country. Most of "Andrews' Raiders" earned their country's highest military decoration, but their commander did not because he was a civilian.

Even so, Andrews made history for leading a group of Yankee spies on a daring raid into Georgia, where, dressed as civilians, they hijacked a locomotive and tore up railroad tracks. It was dubbed the "Great Locomotive Chase." Four movies were based on the story.

In the end, the Rebels captured Andrews and his raiders. They hanged eight of them as spies, including Andrews, a Flemingsburg music teacher and house painter before the war.

The thirty-three-year-old Andrews aimed to disrupt the 138-mile Western & Atlantic Railroad, a vital communications and supply line between Atlanta and Chattanooga. Andrews planned to steal a locomotive and race to Chattanooga, burning bridges behind him. He expected the Union army to capture Chattanooga by the time he arrived.

Andrews was a Virginia native who settled in Flemingsburg in 1859. His two-story red-painted brick house, located near the courthouse, survives. A state historical society marker next to the home relates his storied raid, "a dramatic incident of the Civil War" according to the metal sign.

Andrews chose twenty-three men—another civilian and twenty-two Ohio soldiers, according to the *New Georgia Encyclopedia*. Dressed in civilian clothes, they headed south.

All but two raiders managed to slip through Rebel lines to Marietta, twenty miles north of Atlanta. They claimed to be from Flemingsburg on the way to join the Confederate army.

Seventeen raiders and their commander—Andrews reputedly sported a top hat, gold watch chain and fancy cutaway coat—boarded a Chattanooga-bound train that left Marietta at 5:15 a.m. on April 12, 1862. Two raiders missed the train.

Pulled by the General, a fifty-three-ton steam engine, the train soon stopped at Kennesaw, then called Big Shanty. While everybody else got off for a quick breakfast, the raiders, three of whom were locomotive engineers, swiped the train and sped away.

The Rebels chased the Yankees with a hand-powered pole car and a trio of locomotives, the last one, the Texas, running in reverse. The Texas and the General reportedly reached speeds up to sixty-five miles per hour.

The Andrews house in Flemingsburg. *Photo by the author.*

The monument to the raiders. *Photo by the author.*

The Andrews tombstone. *Photo by the author.*

The raiders tried to thwart their pursuers by ripping up rails, tossing crossties on the tracks and sending a blazing boxcar hurtling at the enemy. The Texas kept coming.

The "Great Locomotive Chase" ended about 1:00 p.m. after the General ran out of wood and water at Ringgold, twenty-three miles short of Chattanooga, which Union forces did not capture until 1863.

The Texas is on display at the famous Atlanta Cyclorama. Said to be the world's largest oil painting, the circular artwork depicts the Civil War battle of Atlanta.

The eight-wheeled General, painted bright red and black, is the featured attraction at the Southern Museum of Civil War and Locomotive History at Kennesaw.

Andrews and the other executed raiders were reburied at the Chattanooga National Cemetery after the Civil War. Individual headstones mark their graves, which are grouped around a large stone pillar topped by a bronze replica of the General.

The Western & Atlantic retired the General in the 1880s. The engine was rebuilt in 1893 and put on display in Chattanooga at the Union Station, where it was a popular tourist attraction. The locomotive came to Kennesaw in 1972.

"If I Were a Poker Player, I'd Sure Hate to Play a 'Stovepipe Johnson'"

It must have been the Civil War's biggest bluff.

Rebel Captain Adam Rankin Johnson of Henderson needed guns for his poorly armed Rebel recruits. He heard about a big cache of Yankee weapons. Trouble was, the firepower was located across the Ohio River in Newburgh, Indiana. More than three hundred Yankees were in the neighborhood.

Johnson had just twenty-seven soldiers. To even the odds, he built a pair of "cannons." He aimed them at Newburgh and scared the Yankees into giving up the muskets. Johnson's "cannoneers" didn't fire a shot. They couldn't have anyway. One of the cannons was a sooty old stovepipe. The other was a fire-blackened log.

Virginia Confederates boasted of "Stonewall" Jackson. Rebel Kentuckians bragged about "Stovepipe" Johnson.

"The employment of sham cannon at the capture of Newburg[h] served to amuse our people, and some wag referred to me as 'stovepipe' Johnson—a title which seemed to so tickle the fancy of the Southern sympathizers that they took it up and spread it far and wide throughout Kentucky and the South," Johnson wrote in *The Partisan Rangers of the Confederate States Army*, his memoirs. "This sobriquet, at first facetiously applied, has stuck to me, and I am distinguished by it to this day."

Not counting places in border state Kentucky, Newburgh was the first town on Union soil that the Confederates bagged. Official records essentially back up Johnson's version of how he bamboozled the bluecoats.

In mid-1862, General John C. Breckinridge of Lexington sent Johnson and Lieutenant Bob Martin, a Muhlenberg countian, on a recruiting trip to their native western Kentucky. At first, they managed to sign up only one man, Frank Amplias Owen.

Apparently, Johnson figured a little publicity might help. So he, Martin and Owen attacked Henderson's eighty-man Union garrison. Johnson and his two-man army sneaked into his hometown after dark on June 29. They crept up to Yankee headquarters, a two-story brick house, and hid behind a plank fence.

A double-barreled blast from Johnson's scattergun began the "Battle" of Henderson. The Union troops scrambled for cover inside the house.

Left: Johnson's CO, General John C. Breckinridge. *Courtesy of the Library of Congress.*

Below: Browning Springs. *Photo by the author.*

The Rebel trio dashed around the house, firing at will. After a while, they leisurely left town for a farm "where we soundly slept till morning," Johnson wrote. He said that the Yankees were too demoralized to send a man out to determine "the numbers of their antagonists." Instead, they "blindly fired out of the upper windows all night at the imaginary foes."

Johnson wrote that Yankee bullets struck a sow. "As she moved about, here and there lying down, leaving blood all around, these fine marksmen claimed they had hit many a rebel, who, either dead or wounded had been taken off the sanguinary field by their comrades."

The "Battle" of Henderson grabbed headlines in the *Evansville Journal*, which Johnson quoted: "Bloody War on the Border! Provost Guard Attacked by Three Hundred Guerrillas. After a Desperate Resistance of over Nine Hours They Succeed in Driving the Enemy off with Heavy Loss! Captain Daily, Lieutenant Lyon and Nine Privates Wounded."

Johnson's report to Breckinridge said that the trio fired eleven shots. He added that they killed a lieutenant and wounded two more officers and nine enlisted men, according to the report (the *Official Records*).

After his Henderson foray, Johnson increased his band to six men. Besides Martin and Owen they were Jake Bennett, Tom Gooch, John Connelly and Marion Myers.

This "Army of Six" routed a three-hundred-man Union cavalry force in nearby Madisonville, the Hopkins County seat. A state historical marker commemorates the spot at the old Browning Springs. Walled in with concrete, the springs still bubble from below the plaque in front of Browning Springs Middle School.

Again, Johnson sprung a night attack. He said he fired first, hitting two Union soldiers and causing others to run from a barn. "The rush of these men, followed by our yelling and shooting, carried terror and dismay into the camp, and the Federals fled wildly into the woods, leaving us in possession of the camp," he wrote.

He admitted to Breckinridge that his band was "not strong enough to take advantage of our victory." Also in his memoirs, Johnson claimed that the Yankees came back and "finding [the cornfield]…full of tracks they themselves had made the day before they gave us credit for a force of fifteen hundred men."

In the days that followed, Johnson added about twenty more men to his force. He named his outfit the "Breckinridge Guards" in honor of his commander.

Meanwhile, the Union cavalry force—which had been sent to Madisonville to burn the homes of Southern sympathizers, according to the historical marker—rode to Henderson, boarded a steamboat and left for Louisville, from whence they came, Johnson wrote. The next day, he added, officials met him outside Henderson and surrendered the town.

"The whole delegation was composed of true friends of the Confederacy," he wrote. "The mayor of the city, Ed. Hall, was afterwards one of my captains. The county judge, Luke Trafton, although he had but one arm, became one of my quartermasters. The Hon. John Young Brown, who was afterwards governor of the State, was one of the party. They all seemed astonished at the small number of men with me."

The Southern sympathizers warned Johnson that a Union gunboat was nearby. Undaunted, he led his troops into the city and hoisted a Rebel flag over the courthouse.

The gunboat skipper sent one of his crew to warn Johnson that he would shell Henderson if the banner was not hauled down. "I determined that the flag should float as long as I occupied the town, so I kept the envoy until I was ready to leave, then moved out just before dark with the flag flying at the head of my little army," Johnson wrote.

From Henderson, Johnson and the Breckinridge Guards rode up the river toward Newburgh. "I was informed there were hundred of stands of guns in the arsenal," Johnson explained in his book.

The weapons were stored in a two-story brick warehouse next to the river. The building belonged to the local Home Guard commander, the aptly named Captain Union Bethell.

Johnson said that he sold Martin on a Newburgh raid. D-Day would be July 18.

Johnson mustered his troops, giving them a chance to back out of the "dangerous enterprise." He declared, "Soldiers, as soon as you reach the other side of the Ohio, you will be standing upon a powder magazine, and cowardice would be the match to ignite it. All who are willing and confident take a step to the front." Johnson wrote that every man "made one step forward."

Assured that his men were with him, Johnson went to work on his two-gun "battery." He scrounged two pairs of old wagon wheels and axles, a stovepipe and a fire-blackened log. He said that he converted the junk into "two of the most formidable-looking pieces of artillery into whose gaping mouths a scared people ever looked."

His "cannons" trained on Newburgh from Scuffletown Beach, Johnson prepared his assault. He and two men would hit Newburgh in a rowboat.

Martin would cross with the rest in commandeered skiffs and the Newburgh ferry.

"We entered the town with 28 men," Johnson reported to Breckinridge. The capture was bloodless; Johnson and his two sidekicks arrived unnoticed. They just walked into the warehouse. However, it didn't take the locals long to realize that enemy soldiers were in town. Peering out from the warehouse, Johnson spied several unarmed men running toward a hotel, which had been turned into a Union military hospital. Johnson decided to "go and quiet their fears."

When Johnson, packing only his shotgun, entered the hotel, he said he "looked upon about eighty men, with their rifles cocked, all ready to fire," he wrote. "The muzzles of the cocked rifles of the front rank were in my face; hesitation meant failure and death."

Johnson added, "Commanding them in a loud voice not to fire a gun or snap a cap, I pushed against the rifles of the front rank with my shotgun and walked right in among them, telling them if they put down their guns before my men came in not one of them should be hurt." Meekly, the Hoosiers complied, stacking their arms, he wrote.

"Urging the whole crowd of them up the stairs, I drove them into a large dining-room at the head of the steps, and taking my place in the doorway with my gun, I bid them keep quiet," Johnson wrote. He added that he soon captured an officer, "a superb specimen of manhood" who "went reluctantly among his men."

Johnson confessed that he was relieved when Martin and his two dozen men arrived. After the Confederates began collecting the weapons for their trip "to Dixie," Johnson said that he learned that Home Guards "representing as being two hundred and fifty strong" were near Newburgh and preparing to liberate the town.

Their commander, Colonel Union Bethell, was in Newburgh. Coolly, Johnson walked up to the Yankee officer "and several excited citizens" and played out his grand bluff.

"I came here to get these guns, I have them and propose to keep them," Johnson claimed he told Bethell. "I want nothing more and do not intend to disturb any of the citizens or any of their property, but if I am hindered or fired on, I'll shell this town to the ground."

Bethell had a spyglass. Johnson invited him to focus it on the Henderson County beach and "see that I am prepared to carry out my threat." Bethell spotted Johnson's "cannons," shot a worried glance at his warehouse and nearby home and "sent his runners at once to stop his men from coming in," Johnson wrote.

Meanwhile, Martin was crossing the river with the last boatload of Yankee ordnance. The raiders also plundered the town of horses, food and other supplies, reportedly with the help of pro-Southern Newburgh residents.

Johnson admitted that he and his two-man "body guard…made the water foam" while escaping in their rowboat. "We were hardly half way across the river when the whole town was swarming with the home guards," he wrote. "They shot down two of their own citizens, but never fired a shot at us, our terrible cannons keeping them in order."

"Stovepipe" told Breckinridge that he made off with "520 muskets, 400 pistols, 150 sabers, and a large lot of commissary and hospital stores." He also said he "paroled 180 prisoners."

Union sources claimed that the haul was less. No matter—Johnson was jubilant. "There is a fine field for operation in this country," he reported to Breckinridge, also claiming that his men "were the pioneer invaders of the Northern soil."

Eventually, Johnson's command grew into the Tenth Kentucky Partisan Rangers. He made general and survived the war, though he was accidentally shot and blinded by his own men in a skirmish in Caldwell County in 1864.

Living in Texas before the war, Johnson returned to the Lone Star State afterward and founded the town of Marble Falls. He died in 1922 at age eighty-eight.

"I HAVE BEEN BRUTALLY MURDERED"

Did the president of the Confederacy really sneak into a Louisville hotel and gun down a Yankee general? When news of General William O. Nelson's slaying broke, some people believed that Jeff Davis did it, according to *City of Conflict*.

A Davis did do it, said George H. Yater, a Louisville historian and author. "There were two Jefferson Davises," he explained. "One was president of the Confederacy. The other was a Union general."

General Jefferson C. Davis shot and killed "Bull" Nelson at the old Galt House. A state historical society marker at Second and Main Streets, the hotel site, commemorates the 1862 assassination, one of the strangest episodes in America's bloodiest war.

Nelson, from Maysville, was a big target at six feet, four inches and three hundred pounds. "He was said to be pretty mean and nasty-tempered, too," said Yater, who wrote *Two Hundred Years at the Falls of the Ohio: A History of Louisville and Jefferson County*. Nelson seemed to hate Hoosiers. Davis was from Indiana. The two started feuding after the Confederates invaded Kentucky in 1862.

Nelson was Louisville's commander. He charged Davis, who was under him, with incompetence. But Davis wasn't the only Hoosier brass hat stung by Nelson's wrath. Nelson claimed that another Indiana general's "stupidity and disobedience" lost the 1862 Battle of Richmond to the Rebels. Nelson was wounded in the fight.

Nelson also tried to hound an Indiana colonel out of the army, claiming that the officer had "pusillanimously" run from the Rebels in a scrap at Lexington, McDowell wrote.

General William O. Nelson. *Courtesy of the Kentucky Historical Society.*

Never mind that Davis's parents were Bluegrass State–born. Nelson claimed that Indiana was inhabited by "uncouth descendants of 'poor trash' from the mountains of Kentucky, Tennessee and North Carolina," according to McDowell.

Davis confronted Nelson at the Galt House on September 29, 1862. With him were Indiana Governor Oliver P. Morton, a powerful political ally of Lincoln, and Thomas W. Gibson, a Louisville lawyer and Indiana native, McDowell added.

Davis told Nelson that he had insulted him. He demanded satisfaction from the Kentucky giant. "Go away, you damned puppy," Nelson roared, according to McDowell. "I don't want anything to do with you." Davis flipped a crumpled hotel card in Nelson's face. Nelson slapped Davis and then walked toward the stairs.

Enraged, Davis grabbed Gibson's pistol and shot the unarmed Nelson in the chest. Nelson managed to climb the steps but collapsed at the top. "Send for a clergyman," McDowell quoted the general's dying whisper. "I wish to be baptized. I have been brutally murdered."

Nelson died minutes later.

Davis pled self-defense, though Nelson was weaponless. He was briefly jailed but released and restored to duty. He fought in several battles and survived the war.

Kentucky Unionists were outraged when Davis was not punished for shooting Nelson. They charged that the Hoosier got away with murder thanks to his friend Morton, who used his political pull to prevent a trial. McDowell said that the governor helped perpetrate a "cold-blooded and cynical miscarriage of justice." He praised Nelson as a hero who was "murdered with impunity."

"SURRENDER IN TWO SECONDS, OR I WILL BLOW YOUR D----D HEAD OFF"

There are no monuments or historical markers in New Haven commemorating what Eastham Tarrant called "one of the most cool and skillful military exploits that happened during the war."

Tarrant might have been biased. He was in on it.

On the night of September 29, 1862, Tarrant's outfit, the First Kentucky Cavalry—dubbed "the Wild Riders"—captured the Third Georgia Cavalry without firing a shot.

The captors were led by a twenty-two-year-old captain who threatened to blow the Confederate commander's head off if he didn't surrender. Colonel Martin J. Crawford complied to Captain Silas Adams.

The "Battle" of New Haven didn't make it into most history books. Tarrant, an ex-sergeant, recounted the bloodless victory in his book, *The Wild Riders of the First Kentucky Cavalry*.

"It was a most critical undertaking," Tarrant wrote.

The Georgia horsemen were part of a large Confederate force that had invaded Kentucky in the late summer of 1862. The First Kentucky was helping defend the state against the Rebels. The regiment was camped at Elizabethtown, about twenty miles from New Haven, when the Yankee brass "was informed by a loyal citizen of the situation of the Georgia regiment," Tarrant recalled.

He added that "a plan was formed for taking it in out of the weather, for it was too late in the season for thinly clad Southerners to be exposed to the chilly night air."

Guided by the informant and joined by the Second Indiana Cavalry, the First Kentucky rode off "about 9 o'clock in the silent hours of night, so as to reach the picket-post of the enemy by daylight on the morning of the 29th," Tarrant wrote.

Adams, according to Tarrant, "had now gained considerable reputation as a dashing, daring officer, and always equal to any emergency in critical situations." So Colonel Frank Wolford, who commanded the First Kentucky and the expedition, put Adams and his men in the front of the force "with orders to charge in column, and, if possible, to capture the enemy without bloodshed."

Shortly before sunup, Union cavalrymen neared the Confederate camp. Four of Adams's men spurred their horses toward a pair of pickets who mistook the dust-covered bluecoats for their own men trying to scare them, Tarrant wrote.

Other troopers captured all but a few of the other Rebel pickets without firing a shot.

Adams ordered a charge, and the Wild Riders "thundered through the wooden bridge across the Rolling Fork, and on through and beyond the surprised and frightened village," Tarrant wrote. "The front companies passed by the camp and surrounded it, while the rear ones halted and 'fronted into line,' and commenced scouring the camp, demanding the surrender of the astonished Rebels, many of whom had not left their tents."

Crawford was asleep in his tent when Adams barged in and demanded he get up. "Who in the h--l are you, giving me such peremptory orders?" Tarrant quoted Crawford, and then he recounted the rest of the exchange between captor and captive:

> "I am commanding the First Kentucky Cavalry," was the reply.
> "But what is your rank?" sternly demanded the "Goober State" Colonel.
> "I am a Captain in command of a regiment, but I have no time to quibble about rank."
> "But let me have a few minutes to consider."
> "Surrender in two seconds, or I will blow your d----d head off,' was Adams's reply.

Tarrant concluded that the enemy was so completely surprised "that not a gun was fired, and every man was captured except a small picket-post on the Bardstown road, and they were chased a short distance." The Yankees gave up the pursuit because a brigade of Rebel infantry was reported in the direction the Southerners were fleeing.

"The Georgians, who had been made believe that if ever they fell into the hands of the heathenish Yankees, that they would be roughly treated, if not murdered, were so highly pleased with the kind treatment of their captors, that they soon became sociable, and did not appear to regret so much being taken by surprise," Tarrant also wrote.

He explained:

> *The Author would here remark, that owing to the men of the regiment having gained a reputation of having but little respect for "red tape," and a contempt for military dudes, many of the Federal army had gotten it into their heads that they mostly belonged to the under stratum of society. This was a great mistake; for while not a great many belonged to the polished aristocracy, the great mass of the regiment belonged to the sterling yeomanry of the land, and made it a universal practice, with some few exceptions, of treating those of the enemy who fell into their hands with courtesy and humanity.*

"I'll Be Damned if This Is Not Getting Rather Particular"

Congressman James Streshly Jackson of Hopkinsville wanted to do more in the Civil War than pass laws and make patriotic speeches.

He joined the Union army and gave his life in the bloodiest battle ever fought on Kentucky soil. A general who purportedly "possessed great personal attractions," Jackson was among the slain at Perryville on October 8, 1862. He was thirty-nine.

"Well, I'll be damned if this is not getting rather particular," the mustachioed Jackson reputedly growled as some of his men retreated in a hail of enemy fire. Noticing one of their officers on horseback, Jackson warned him to dismount, lest he be killed. But it was Jackson who fell, shot through the chest.

Jackson was one of several House members who resigned from the Thirty-seventh Congress to don Yankee blue. The western Kentuckian was evidently the only lawmaker who died in combat.

Even so, Jackson is not widely known, even in Hopkinsville, where he is buried at old Riverside Cemetery. The general is not in the *Kentucky Encyclopedia*, nor does he rate much ink in Bluegrass State history books.

A Fayette County native, Jackson also served in the Mexican-American War, where he battled more than Mexican soldiers. Lieutenant Jackson fought a duel with Captain Thomas F. Marshall, a fellow Kentucky officer. Neither man was hurt, but Jackson reputedly resigned from the army to escape a court-martial.

A lawyer in civilian life, Jackson settled in Hopkinsville in 1859. Shortly after the Civil War began in 1861, second district voters elected him to Congress on the Union ticket.

Jackson left his seat to help recruit the Third Kentucky Cavalry, which he commanded as a colonel in the Battle of Shiloh. Later, he became a general under Lincoln's "policy of rewarding loyal border-state politicians with higher rank, whatever their military qualifications," according to *Generals in Blue* by Ezra J. Warner.

General James S. Jackson. *Courtesy of the Kentucky Historical Society.*

Warner said that Jackson evidently deserved promotion. The soldier-politician ended up leading an infantry division in battle at Perryville, a small Boyle County town. Jackson was among about 7,500 Union and Confederate troops killed or wounded in the fierce fighting.

Jackson died on a hilltop near a Union artillery battery, according to Kurt Holman, manager of Perryville Battlefield State Historic Site. "Apparently, he was on foot," Holman added.

Colonel Samuel M. Starling, also of Hopkinsville, and others rushed to help Jackson, according to *Perryville: This Grand Havoc of Battle* by Kenneth Noe. They were too late. Starling found Jackson's "eyes…closed, with a tightness preternatural." The bullet that killed him tore "a hole in his coat surrounded by blood ½ an inch all around it," the colonel reported.

General Don Carlos Buell's Yankee army and General Braxton Bragg's Rebel forces fought one another to a standstill at Perryville. But the battle is considered a Union victory because Bragg retreated from Kentucky, thus all but ending Confederate hopes of prying the loyal state out of the Union.

"THE IRONY IS INCREDIBLE"

Nobody tried harder to prevent the Civil War than Henry Clay of Lexington.

Even so, America's bloodiest conflict ended up in his backyard. "Literally," said Kent Masterson Brown, a Lexington historian and author.

On October 18, 1862, Rebels and Yankees battled in the woods behind Ashland, Clay's Lexington mansion, which is preserved as a museum at 120 Sycamore Road. "The irony is incredible," added Brown, who also practices law in the Fayette County seat.

Dubbed the "Great Pacificator," Clay is famous for three compromises he hoped would save the Union and stave off war between the North and South. He didn't live to see the shootout in his woodlot; Clay died ten years earlier.

General John Hunt Morgan of Lexington led the Rebels. Hopemont, his home, is also a museum at 201 North Mill Street in Lexington's historic Gratz Park.

Most of "Morgan's Raiders" were Kentuckians. Ohioans were their foes when they galloped into Lexington. Morgan had about 1,800 men.

General John Hunt Morgan. *Courtesy of the Kentucky Historical Society.*

The Yankees, troopers from the Third and Fourth Ohio Cavalry Regiments, evidently numbered about 300.

Apparently, the Union brass wasn't expecting trouble. Leaving their men bivouacked in Clay's woods, several officers checked into the Phoenix Hotel downtown.

Morgan struck at dawn. "The affair was over in about ten minutes," Brown said. The Confederates killed four Union soldiers. The rest, including two dozen wounded, surrendered.

Brown said that twenty Confederates were wounded. "Mostly from friendly fire," he added.

Cavalrymen led by two of Morgan's top officers, Basil W. Duke and W.C.P. Breckinridge, sandwiched the Ohioans in a "slight depression," according to Duke's *History of Morgan's Cavalry*. "I got the benefit of Breckinridge's fire—in great part at least. I saw a great cloud of white smoke suddenly puff out and rise like a wall pierced by flashes of flame, and the next instant the balls came whizzing through my column, fortunately killing no one. This volley settled the enemy and repulsed me!"

Morgan's men bagged a few more prisoners at the hotel and the Fayette County Courthouse. "We don't know exactly how many Union troops were in Lexington, but Morgan captured about three hundred," Brown said.

The general paroled his captives and sent them off toward Louisville, minus their weapons, boots and horses. "He left town about 1:00 p.m.," Brown said.

Morgan had to depart without his cousin, Major George Washington Morgan. "A retreating Union trooper shot him in the throat," Brown said. Both men died, the Union soldier evidently on the spot. "Wash" Morgan succumbed a few days later at Hopemont. Morgan was killed at Greenville, Tennessee, in 1864.

A bronze equestrian statue of Morgan stands in front of the old Fayette County Courthouse, now the Lexington History Museum, at 215 West Main Street. The likeness was dedicated on October 18, 1911, the anniversary of the "Battle of Ashland," Brown said.

CANNONBALL STUCK IN A WALL IS A TOURIST ATTRACTION IN ELIZABETHTOWN

A souvenir of Morgan's famous "Christmas Raid" of 1862 is stuck in a brick wall in Elizabethtown.

Left: Elizabethtown's "cannonball in the wall." *Photo by the author.*

Below: Close-up of the cannonball. *Photo by the author.*

Morgan and his men struck on December 27, pumping 107 cannon rounds into the city and killing or wounding several of its outnumbered Yankee defenders.

A cannonball plowed into the old Depp Building on the court square. Twenty-five years later, the building burned down and was restored, ultimately with the cannonball back in place. Painted black, the iron cannonball is half-embedded in the blue-painted brick several feet above the sidewalk.

A bronze plaque fastened to the wall reads: "Civil War Cannon Ball Below Upper Window. Fired From Cemetery by Morgan's Men." If that's not plain enough, a black metal arrow points toward the metal missile, which looks to be about five inches in diameter.

Tourists and other visitors to the Hardin County seat often stop and take photos of the cannonball. A sidewalk sign describes it and Morgan's attack on the town.

About 650 Federal troops defended the town against Morgan's 3,900 horsemen. The Union troops "set up a strong resistance," wrote Edison H. Thomas in *John Hunt Morgan and His Raiders*. "For protection they had fortified a number of brick warehouses near the railroad station, complete with loopholes through which they could aim rifles."

Morgan surrounded the town, posted his artillery on cemetery hill about a mile south of where the cannonball landed and ordered the Yankees to give up. When they refused, Morgan's gunners opened fire, the sign notes. "The bombardment, along with a quick 'cavalry' charge on foot along the streets, soon convinced the enemy that Morgan meant business, and they surrendered," Thomas wrote.

After paroling their captives, Morgan and his men galloped off to destroy two railroad trestles at nearby Muldraugh Hill. "Elizabethtown residents went to work repairing the damage inflicted by the missiles," according to the sign.

The cannonball remained a reminder of the Civil War until an 1887 fire destroyed the city block that included the Depp Building. The cannonball ended up buried in the charred rubble.

Miss Annie Nourse asked the Depp Building owners if she could have the old relic, according to the sidewalk sign. They agreed. Nourse offered a twenty-five-cent reward to any local lad who mined the cannonball from the debris and brought it to her, according to the sidewalk sign. "A lively scramble instantly ensued in the pile of hot bricks," Nourse was quoted in a 1932 newspaper article, part of which is reprinted on the sign. "I left them digging and went home. In the afternoon, a *man* brought it to me and demanded $5.00 for it. I told him it was already mine. After some hesitation he decided to leave it for 50 cents, which I gave him."

Ultimately, the buildings were reconstructed. Eventually, somebody decided that the cannonball ought to be put back. Nourse was happy to oblige, according to the sign. By then, the Depp Building was a bank. (It is now a law office.) "Many years after...I restored [the cannonball] to the bank and they had it placed in the same spot, as near as possible [in the new building], where it is seen today."

"I...Will Gallop Up One [of] These Days ...and Call on You for that Good Dinner of Which You Spoke"

Sergeant G.W. Hurt's Christmas wasn't merry.

He wrote his family, admitting he was afraid that "some list of casualties... will bear my name like a dagger to the hearts of those who love me."

Hurt, who was from near Mayfield, was with the Confederate army close to Murfreesboro, Tennessee, in December 1862. His letter was dated December 27, just before the Battle of Stones River. The battle was named for a boulder-strewn stream that winds through the middle Tennessee town.

Lon Carter Barton owned some of Hurt's letters. He said that Hurt joined the Southern forces in 1861. Hurt's letters could have been written by any soldier in any war. Their themes are universal. In the letter Barton prized most, Hurt wanted to explain a battle to relatives who had never experienced combat. Most veterans say that this is impossible. But Hurt tried.

"The loud roar of the first big guns, as it reverberates from hill to hill tells the hour has come," wrote Hurt, who received his baptism of fire at Fort Donelson. "Then a sharp skirmish, then the dread of the general engagement."

Hurt aimed to reassure his family. "I am not anxious to fight but when it is necessary I can go into it calm and without fear." He ended his letter by changing to a cheerier subject. "What sort of a Christmas have you had, a very pleasant one?"

Hurt was lucky to be alive. He had written home about the smaller Battle of Hartsville, Tennessee, on December 7, 1862. Yankee fire had decimated his regiment, the Second Kentucky Infantry. Hurt was in Company D, a Graves County outfit.

"Our Regt. carried three hundred and seventy five men into the fight [the Second Kentucky began the war with about one thousand men] and our killed and wounded were about seventy," he wrote. Hurt was not hit in the Hartsville battle, but he wrote that a bullet slashed the bayonet scabbard from his belt.

Hurt evaded death at the Battle of Stones River (fought from December 31, 1862, to January 2, 1863) and other battles that followed. He wrote home from Georgia in 1864, telling his family that the Second Kentucky—part of the "Orphan Brigade"—was about to become mounted infantry. In that letter, Hurt promised his loved ones a surprise. "I...will gallop up one [of] these days, when you are not thinking about it and call on you for that good dinner of which you spoke."

His promise was not kept. Hurt was badly wounded at the Battle of Jonesboro, Georgia, near Atlanta, on September 1, 1864. Twenty days later, Sergeant G.W. Hurt was dead.

"Their Faces Toward Heaven, Their Feet to the Foe"

While G.W. Hurt survived Stones River, many Kentuckians on both sides did not.

Eight Union soldiers from the Bluegrass State were buried on the battlefield next to one of the oldest Civil War memorials.

Union troops built the Hazen Brigade Monument to their fallen comrades. The old cairn is a landmark on the Stones River National Battlefield near Murfreesboro.

Fifty-five graves flank the historic memorial. The epitaph reads: "Hazen's Brigade to the Memory of Its Soldiers Who Fell at Stone River Dec. 31, 1862 'Their Faces Toward Heaven, Their Feet to the Foe.'" The flat-topped, "quadrangular pyramidal shaft" is eleven feet tall and ten feet square.

Colonel William B. Hazen's brigade, including the Sixth Kentucky Infantry, was the only Union outfit not to give ground to fierce Confederate attacks on December 31. His brigade suffered more than four hundred casualties.

The Hazen Monument. *Photo by the author.*

A Kentucky soldier's grave. *Photo by the author.*

The three-day Battle of Stones River ended in Union victory. Union General William S. Rosecrans forced General Braxton Bragg to withdraw his Rebel army from the stony, cedar-studded battlefield, 650 acres of which are preserved in the park.

"The Union army stayed in the area for quite a while after the battle," said Gib Backlund, director of park operations. "That gave Hazen's men time to build the monument."

Hundreds of Kentucky troops fought under Rosecrans or Bragg in the Battle of Stones River. On January 2, Hazen's men helped repel the charge of Hurt and his "Orphan Brigade" comrades. Bragg retreated on January 3.

Buried at the Hazen Monument are Privates Franz Bassell, Charles Hitner, Joseph Kram, John Matly, Joseph Maas, Adam Maus (or Moas), James Mulberry and Bernhard Schneller. They served in the Sixth Kentucky, one of Hazen's four regiments.

Also inscribed on the monument are the names of Colonel Walter Whitaker, Lieutenant Colonel George T. Cotten and Captain Charles S. Todd. Whitaker, who was promoted to general, was the Sixth Kentucky's first commander. Cotten and Todd were killed in the battle, but they were buried in Kentucky.

Two other Sixth Kentucky soldiers killed at Stones River lie in unknown graves. They are Corporal Henry C. Cardwell and Private Joshua McKee.

Chiseled on the monument, too, are names of brigade officers who perished in the Battle of Shiloh in April 1862. Second Lieutenant Anton Hand of the Sixth Kentucky is on the roll of the dead.

The monument stands where Hazen's brigade defended a little wood known as the Round Forest. The Union troops dubbed the killing ground "Hell's Half Acre." The monument is surrounded by a stone wall. There are tombstones for about half of the graves inside the enclosure.

Organized in 1861 with about nine hundred men, the Sixth Kentucky mainly came from Louisville and central and northern Kentucky counties. Besides Shiloh and Stones River, the regiment fought at Chickamauga, Chattanooga, Kennesaw Mountain and in the battles around Atlanta. Only about three hundred men were on regimental rolls when the war ended, according to historian Joe Reinhart.

"A Cannon Invented by a Kentuckian and Captured by a Kentuckian"

Union Captain Reuben Patrick's Civil War trophy is one of the rarest relics at the Kentucky Military History Museum in Frankfort, the state capital.

"It's a cannon invented by a Kentuckian and captured by a Kentuckian," said Bill Bright, curator of the museum. "We're lucky to have it."

In March 1863, Patrick, thirty-three, single-handedly swiped the Williams Rapid Fire Gun from Confederates camped close to Ivyton in his native Magoffin County.

"On night of 20th, as posted guards slept, Patrick boldly detached gun from carriage, hid it in woods," explains a state historical marker on Kentucky Highway 1888 at Patrick's Magoffin County grave site. Thus deprived of their only artillery, the Rebels moved on, forsaking the carriage, the marker adds.

Not many Civil War weapons are scarcer than Williams Guns, Bright said. Few of the lightweight cannons were made, evidently all of them in Richmond, Virginia, the Rebel capital.

"Basically, the Williams Gun was the first automatic weapon produced in the United States," John Trowbridge said. "It was a design ahead of its time." Williams, apparently from Covington, is all but forgotten, Bright said.

"We're not even sure about his first name. In old records, he is called 'R.S. Williams,' 'D.R.S. Williams' and even 'Dr. R.S. Williams.'"

Patrick, an officer in the Fourteenth Kentucky Infantry Regiment, led a Yankee detachment against the Rebels at Ivyton, according to the historical marker. Another marker near Salyersville, the Magoffin County seat, notes that the Fourteenth Kentucky "operated in this area to scout and protect east Ky."

Patrick was born in 1830 at Burning Fork in Magoffin County, county library records show. Perhaps because he was a gun-grabbing hero, Magoffin voters elected Patrick to the state House of Representatives in 1863 and 1865, according to *A History of Kentucky* by Lewis and Richard Collins.

After the Civil War, the Williams Gun decorated the Magoffin County Courthouse lawn. Later, it was displayed at the home of one of Patrick's great-grandsons, library records also reveal.

Only the small-bore cannon's skinny, seven-foot, black iron barrel is at the military museum, which is housed in the old state arsenal, a two-story, 1850-vintage red brick building that looks like a castle. Bright said that the

Williams Gun was designed to shoot up to sixty one-pound projectiles per minute, but he doubts the weapon ever did.

"It's a weird-looking contraption," Trowbridge said. "Shells were fed into the cannon from a magazine on top of the barrel. It was fired by turning a huge crank, similar to a Gatling gun."

Evidently, the Williams Guns were prone to jamming when they got hot. "They were probably more dangerous to their crews than to the enemy," Trowbridge said.

"The Trip Contemplated Was Perilous in the Extreme"

Margaret G. Vaughn of Garrard County had two sons away at war in the First Kentucky Union Cavalry. She didn't appreciate Rebel officers bragging about how their little army was making fools of the Yankees, including her offspring.

"They were laughing at their success in spreading false reports in regard to their strength, and causing the Union forces to retreat, when they could easily have driven them back, as the Federals were much the stronger," she recalled in *The Wild Riders.*

So Vaughn enlisted Louisa West Jackman of Lancaster, the Garrard

Louisa West Jackman. *Courtesy of the Kentucky Historical Society.*

County seat, to go with her to tell the Union troops the truth. "The trip contemplated was perilous in the extreme," Tarrant wrote.

The Yankees were across the Kentucky River at Camp Nelson. To reach them, Vaughn and Jackman would have to dodge enemy patrols, descend the steep cliffs that flank the river and somehow cross the rain-swollen waterway.

If not for Tarrant's account, the heroism of "the two loyal ladies" might have been forgotten. But after hearing from Vaughn and Jackman, the Yankees attacked and drove the outmanned and outgunned Rebel raiders away.

The Southerners, according to Tarrant, were stealing "the fine beef cattle and blooded horses from the farmers of Lincoln, Boyle and Garrard counties for Confederate use." Most citizens in the area were Unionists, especially in Lincoln and Garrard Counties.

At 10:00 a.m. on March 26, 1863, Vaughn and Jackman rode away from Lancaster on two horses that Vaughn furnished. Their trip to Union army headquarters wouldn't end until 8:00 p.m., March 27.

According to Tarrant, Vaughn told Jackman that she had been up all night on the twenty-fifth, holding the reins of her horses to prevent the Confederates from taking the animals. She also had unwelcome lodgers at her house—Rebel officers. Vaughn said she overheard them joking about how they were bamboozling the bluecoats.

According to Tarrant, Jackman informed Vaughn that Rebels had "taunted her with the cowardice of the Federal army in retreating before an inferior force; that she had retorted that they would get enough of the Union forces' cowardice before they left the State."

But there was no doubt that the Union brass believed the Confederate forces were much larger than they were. To prevent the Rebels from getting at them, the Yankees had even removed the planks from Hickman Bridge, a long, covered span over the river near Camp Nelson, a large, fortified Union recruit center in Jessamine County. The bridge was to be burned if necessary to stop the Confederates.

One Rebel, according to Vaughn, suggested "that if they could cause the Union forces to burn the Hickman bridge, they could have everything their own way for a few days."

Vaughn and Jackman avoided the main roads, cutting across farm fields and taking "by-ways and mud roads, which were almost impassable," Tarrant wrote. They ended up crossing the river at Polly's Bend "eighteen miles by direct road from Lancaster," he added.

But their trip was far from direct. "By the zig-zag course they were compelled to pursue to avoid the public highways and the enemy, it is uncertain what distance they traveled…in reaching our lines," Tarrant wrote.

First, they had to get across the river, "the most formidable object, perhaps," Tarrant explained. "Its high stage from the previous rains, its rugged cliffs, rising in some places 300 feet high and perpendicular, with only here and there a place of descent from bench to bench, along narrow passways, with overhanging masses of rock on one side, and yawning precipices on the other."

A slave child fleeing the Rebels offered to help them find a place to cross near Hickman Bridge. They went with him, but enemy pickets turned them back. Tarrant didn't say what happened to the child. But after spending the night with friends in Bryantsville, Vaughn and Jackman continued their trek on March 27.

A Rebel colonel on horseback turned them around. After he left, they rode back to the river, evading more pickets.

Vaughn and Jackman found additional aid from local Unionists. Two men helped them down the cliffs. Another man brought a small raft over from the other side of the river. "The current ran strong, the raft sinking so low that the water ran across their feet," Tarrant wrote. "Those on the bank held their breath in awe, expecting to see the precious load go down; but they landed safely, and were joyfully received by the Union pickets."

With the assistance of two soldiers, Vaughn and Jackman commandeered "a topless buggy" and drove it to First Kentucky Cavalry headquarters. They arrived in a pouring rain.

The First Kentucky commander, Colonel Wolford of Liberty, relayed what Vaughn and Jackman told him to General Quincy A. Gillmore. He ordered Wolford and his men to re-lay the bridge planks, enabling the First Kentucky and other Union forces to attack across the span to victory on March 28.

While the Rebels retreated, the enemy wasn't gone from Garrard County for good. Another Southern cavalry force galloped into Lancaster on July 31. Again, a visitor knocked at Jackman's door, but a Southern sympathizer this time. The woman, according to Tarrant, begged Jackman "to accompany her home, telling her that she was sure… [the Confederates] would have her hung."

Jackman, the author added, wouldn't budge. "The brave woman declined the kind invitation, and assured her friend, that if they wanted her, they would find her at home; and if they were simple enough to hang her, Wolford's men would pay them back in their own coin, and would not stop at hanging one, but would clean out the town."

Soon, Union cavalry, led by Captain George W. Dye of the First Kentucky, dashed into Lancaster "capturing and shooting the raiders, when the terrorists at once became the terror-stricken."

"THE COMMENCEMENT OF THIS RAID IS OMINOUS"

The Yankees had just twenty men to defend the Green River Bridge at Tebbs Bend near Campbellsville against two hundred of General John Hunt Morgan's cavalry.

"The night before the battle, they rode horses back and forth across the bridge to make the Confederates think reinforcements were arriving," said Betty Gorin, an author and historian in Campbellsville, the Taylor County seat. "There weren't any reinforcements for thirty miles."

No matter; the Union troops held the little wooden span and helped win the Battle of Tebbs Bend. It was July 4, 1863, the day General Robert E. Lee retreated from Gettysburg and Grant captured Vicksburg. Thus, Tebbs Bend was all but forgotten as a Civil War battle.

Gorin and her group, the Tebbs Bend Battlefield Association, have preserved the site where a total of 220 Yankees defeated about 1,000 Rebels, most of them Kentuckians. "We wanted to honor the men, North and South, who exhibited exceptional qualities of bravery and leadership we all can admire," said Gorin, who wrote *Morgan Is Coming!*, a book about the famous general.

The Battle of Tebbs Bend was not a promising start to Morgan's "Great Raid." "The commencement of this raid is ominous," a Rebel major lamented after the bloody fight. He was a future governor, James B. McCreary of Richmond.

Gorin's nonprofit organization published a pamphlet that outlines a self-guided driving tour of the battlefield. "Visitors have included West Point cadets who were learning the importance of terrain in strongly defended positions," she said.

The tour route winds past signs and markers and a granite shaft erected in 1872 to honor the Confederate dead. Near the monument is a green metal tablet that the State of Michigan put up in tribute to its troops. "Most of the Union soldiers in the battle were from Michigan," Gorin said.

While their comrades in arms held the bridge, another two hundred Union soldiers vanquished eight hundred more Confederates atop limestone bluffs that tower over the river. Colonel O.H. Moore's Yankees were dug in behind earthen breastworks protected by abatis—felled trees whose limbs were interlaced and sharpened.

The bluff top defense line is gone. A red brick house and grassy lawn mark the killing ground.

Before attacking, Morgan dispatched three of his officers to order the outnumbered Union troops to give up. Moore wasted no time on a reply: "Present my compliments to General Morgan and say, this being the fourth of July, I cannot entertain the proposition to surrender."

Eight times the Kentuckians charged the Michigan men, but to no avail. After three and a half hours of combat under a blazing summer sun, Moore ordered a bugle call to make the Confederates believe fresh troops had arrived.

"That completely demoralized the Confederates," Gorin said. "They asked for permission to bury their dead under a flag of truce, then withdrew."

All told, the Confederates lost thirty-six men killed and forty-five wounded. At least thirty Rebels are buried around the monument. Union losses were put at six killed and twenty-four wounded, two of whom later died, Gorin said.

Despite his defeat at Tebbs Bend, Morgan pressed on.

"THE FARTHEST POINT NORTH EVER REACHED BY ANY BODY OF CONFEDERATE TROOPS DURING THE CIVIL WAR"

Morgan's Raiders flew the Rebel flag deeper in Yankee territory than any other Southern soldiers in the Civil War.

"That flag is in our museum," said Steve Munson. "We're proud to have it."

The old "Stars and Bars" was the battle flag of Morgan's famous Second Kentucky Cavalry Regiment. The hand-sewn, red, white and blue banner is a prized relic at the War Memorial of Mid America Museum in Bardstown, the Nelson County seat, according to Munson, a local Civil War historian and relic collector.

Munson and Jack Harrison, also of Bardstown, own the flag. They loaned it to the museum, where they are on the board of directors.

Crossed cavalry sabers and "2ⁿᵈ KY" are also emblazoned in gold paint on the flag. "This is the one Morgan had when he was captured in Ohio in 1863," Munson said.

The Yankees bagged Morgan and 336 of his soldiers near West Point, Ohio, on July 26, 1863. A stone memorial erected in 1909 claimed that the site was "THE FARTHEST POINT NORTH EVER REACHED BY ANY BODY OF CONFEDERATE TROOPS DURING THE CIVIL WAR."

Most of Morgan's men were from the Bluegrass State. Many of their pursuers in blue were Kentuckians. One of their commanders was General James L. Shackleford of Louisville. The museum also has his ivory-handled .44-caliber Colt pistol and dress sword.

Colonel Frank Wolford and the First Kentucky Cavalry were also galloping after Morgan. The First and Second Kentucky Regiments "made each other's acquaintance at a very early period of the war—an acquaintance which continued with scarcely any intermission until the close of the Ohio raid," Duke wrote in *Reminiscences of General Basil W. Duke*. Duke explained:

> The "differences" between these men of these two very active bodies of "light horse," like those of Gabriel and Lucifer in Byron's "Vision of Judgment," were "purely political," and did not seem to affect their personal and "social" relations in the least...Their combats were sharp and closely contested, but the prisoners taken on each side were always treated with the utmost kindness and consideration, until a strange sort of friendship grew up between them. Between Morgan and Wolford especially there was a warm and mutual regard. In our numerous encounters with him "Old Frank" was more than once wounded, as much to our regret perhaps as his own.

Harper's Weekly was not as charitable toward Morgan and his men, who lived off the land.

"The famous bandit levied pretty freely on the defenseless towns and villages," the periodical reported. Union troops killed, wounded or captured most of the Raiders. They cornered Morgan and the remnants of his weary band close to West Point, less than seventy miles south of Lake Erie.

Reputedly, Wolford treated Morgan and his officers to a chicken dinner at a local hotel after they surrendered. Wolford, according to Duke, also "made every effort to have [Morgan]...paroled and exchanged, and on more than one occasion was involved in quarrels with the angry crowds which threatened Morgan on his way to prison."

While Morgan's battle flag survived the war, he didn't. After escaping from the Ohio State Penitentiary in Columbus, where he was locked up as a prisoner of war, Morgan was killed by a Yankee soldier at Greenville, Tennessee, in 1864. Morgan is buried in Lexington Cemetery.

Following the Civil War, an Ohio Grand Army of the Republic post displayed the Second Kentucky flag as a battle trophy, according to Munson. The GAR was a Union veterans' organization similar to the American Legion.

A ONE-MAN ARMY

Jack Hinson swore bloody vengeance when the Yankees executed his two sons as guerrillas near Fort Heiman in Calloway County.

Before he finished his vendetta, he reputedly had ambushed and killed thirty-six Union soldiers. The sniper commemorated the death of each one by filing a notch into his rifle barrel.

Hinson was one of the most feared Confederate guerrillas in what is the Land Between The Lakes (LBL) national recreation area today. In his book *The Land Between the Rivers*, J. Milton Henry called him "the phantom of the river bottoms and swamps" bordering the Tennessee and Cumberland Rivers. His killing ground was the rugged, sparsely settled "Between the Rivers" section of Trigg County and adjacent Stewart County, Tennessee. Allen claimed that the Yankees feared Hinson more than any other "Between the Rivers" guerrilla.

Henry wrote that, by the time the Civil War began in 1861, Hinson was a prosperous Stewart County landowner. His sons were shot, probably in 1862, by Iowa cavalry troopers who had occupied Fort Heiman after the Rebels abandoned the Tennessee River earthwork opposite Fort Henry.

Whether the youths were guerrillas is uncertain. According to *Center of Conflict*, the Hinson boys were merely squirrel hunting near the fort when the Yankees arrested them.

At any rate, Colonel W.W. Lowe, commander of the Fifth Iowa Cavalry, said they were guerrillas. He stood them before a firing squad.

Enraged over the deaths of his sons, "Old Jack," as friends and neighbors knew Hinson, picked up his rifle and began to roam the hills, hollows and riverbanks in search of human quarry. "He had an especial bitterness toward Federal gunboats," Henry wrote. "He would lie in ambush for hours watching for Federal gunboats that were carrying men and supplies along the rivers…Officers and boatmen who wore the blue were special targets for Hinson's deadly rifle. Isolated federal patrols were often attacked by him."

Allen wrote that Hinson knew the country around Fort Heiman. "He used his knowledge to excellent advantage. He would station himself along a spring of water—any place a Yankee soldier was likely to appear. And with a patience born of squirrel hunting, he waited for his prey to appear."

Hinson was also familiar with the Cumberland and Tennessee Rivers. The Tennessee especially was a vital supply line to Union armies farther south. "Where the current brought boats close to the shore, he erected duck blinds from which he could pick off pilots or other men on the Union boats forever plying the Tennessee," Allen wrote.

Union troops scoured the countryside for the sniper. "Since Hinson had lived between the rivers for some 15 years before the Civil War, he was familiar with all the trails and conditions of the area," explained Henry. "He could and did elude many Federal detachments sent out to capture or kill him, and remained a terror to Federal forces."

Frustrated, the Yankees put a price on Hinson's head. There were no takers. Most local citizens were pro-Southern. Hinson's Unionist neighbors feared him, Henry said.

"He threatened the lives of those Union sympathizers and raided their homes when he felt he could get away with it," Henry wrote. "The children of these Union sympathizers long remembered these raids and loathed him as a robber and a thief."

Hinson was doubtless glad for the Confederate company when Forrest's cavalry showed up in 1864. By then, the Yankees had given up Fort Heiman. Forrest's troopers sneaked into the fort and briefly used it to ambush Union supply boats on the Tennessee. Allen wrote that Hinson helped guide the Southerners to the fort.

Hinson survived the Civil War. His bloody career as a sniper was noted on a Kentucky Historical Society marker on U.S. Highway 68 near the highway's junction with the Trace, the LBL's main north–south road.

THE YANKEE CURSER

George McEntire trekked from Texas to Cumberland Gap to honor his grandfather's dying wish. He cursed the Yankees.

"We tell visitors about him," said Janice S. Miracle, a volunteer and former ranger at Cumberland Gap National Historical Park near Middlesboro. "But we don't use any of the colorful metaphors he used," added ranger Matthew Graham.

On September 9, 1863, a Yankee army captured the famous Appalachian mountain pass and its Rebel defenders. The Confederate prisoners of war included Lieutenant William R. McEntire.

The rock on which McEntire carved his name. *Photo by the author.*

The spot where the "Yankee Cusser's" gun battery was stationed. *Photo by the author.*

"In 1917, on his deathbed, he made his young grandson George promise he would return to the Gap on the one hundredth anniversary of his capture, face the North and curse the Yankees for five minutes," Miracle said.

George McEntire kept his word on September 9, 1963.

"He was a kindly old gentleman who came back several times after that, bringing his tall, slender cowboy grandsons," Miracle said. Supposedly, they were to carry on the tradition of cursing the Yankees. "But to my knowledge none of them have returned to date."

The historic gateway to the Bluegrass State in pioneer days, Cumberland Gap was a strategic spot in the Civil War. The mountain pass changed hands several times in America's bloodiest conflict.

McEntire, a Georgia artillery officer, helped defend the gap against Union General Ambrose E. Burnside. Fearing that he was outnumbered, Confederate General John W. Frazer ordered his army to surrender to the Yankees.

McEntire kept firing at the Union soldiers until Frazer had him stopped at gunpoint. Still defiant, McEntire and his men reputedly "took several opportunities" to tear down the Stars and Stripes when the Yankees hoisted the flag over Cumberland Gap, Miracle said.

McEntire helped defend Rebel Fort Pitt—which became Union Fort Lyon—high up on a mountain. Before he capitulated, he carved "W.R. McENTIRE, Liet. Co. A, 9 GA. Bat. Arty, September 9, 1863" on a boulder.

Earthworks and a preserved Civil War cannon mark the site of Fort Pitt-Lyon, which is close to the Pinnacle Overlook. A paved footpath winds between the cannon and the low, flat boulder. McEntire's inscription is hard to make out.

"The '1863' is pretty legible, but the rest of it is pretty faint—maybe 10 percent readable," Graham said.

Burnside shipped his Rebel captives off to prisoner of war camps up north. McEntire survived, migrated to Texas, became a wealthy man and lived into his eighties. "George McEntire, who died in the early '90s, sent me a dozen roses once," Miracle said.

Graham said the Texan's grandfather was true to his Scots-Irish heritage. "He had a temper. He spoke his mind and wasn't bashful at all."

"The Bosom of the Placid, Broad Tennessee River and the Beautiful Valleys Appeared to Shout for Very Joy"

One of the most famous photographs of World War II shows five Marines hoisting the Stars and Stripes over Mount Suribachi during the bloody Battle of Iwo Jima.

There was a similar scene during the Civil War. While no photographer preserved the flag-raising for posterity as it happened, the heroes, a half-dozen Kentuckians, obligingly restaged the event for a photographer a few days later.

On November 25, 1863, Captain John C. Wilson of Estill County and five other soldiers from the Eighth Kentucky Infantry raised Old Glory above the rocky crest of Lookout Mountain, about 1,400 feet above Chattanooga, Tennessee. Thousands of victory-hungry Union troops cheered from the city.

A state historical marker on Kentucky Highway 52 in West Irvine hails Wilson as a "LOOKOUT MOUNTAIN HERO." According to *History of the Eighth Regiment Kentucky Volunteers*, after leading his men to the mountaintop just before dawn, the forty-one-year-old officer "unfurled to the morning breeze that dear old emblem of light and liberty." The old book also notes that "as the sight of the flag met the upturned gaze of our vast army below, cheer after cheer echoed from camp to camp, from mountain to mountain, until the bosom of the placid, broad Tennessee River and the beautiful valleys appeared to shout for very joy."

The prose might be a tad flowery for twenty-first-century readers. But Jim Ogden, historian at the Chickamauga and Chattanooga National Military Park, says that the story is basically true. "The flag-raising was a tremendous psychological boost for the Union Army. Captain Wilson steps onto the point of Lookout Mountain just as the sun comes up."

The Eighth Kentucky, from Estill and nearby counties, was part of General Ulysses S. Grant's forces at Chattanooga. The veteran regiment was in the Army of the Cumberland.

On November 24, the Eighth Kentucky had joined an attack to dislodge part of the Rebel Army of Tennessee from Lookout Mountain, which towers over Chattanooga. The fight was dubbed the "battle above the clouds."

After the battle, there was to be little rest for Captain Wilson and his men, who had survived a hail of enemy bullets and cannon fire. The Union brass wanted to make sure the Rebels were gone.

Early on November 25, General Walter C. Whitaker, a Shelbyville native, sought volunteers from the Eighth Kentucky to scout the mountaintop for the enemy. When Wilson agreed, the general asked the captain to take the regiment's American flag.

The banner had been made "at the beginning of the war [by] the ladies of Estill County…and presented to the…[regiment]," Wilson recalled in Perrin, Battle and Kniffen's 1888 book *Kentucky: A History of the State*. The old soldier said he carried the flag to the top in honor of "the ladies of Estill."

At the same time, General John W. Geary called on soldiers from the Twenty-ninth Pennsylvania to reconnoiter to the crest, but by a different route than the Kentuckians planned to take.

"The ascent became a contest between Easterners and Westerners, and everyone eagerly awaited the result," Peter Cozzens wrote in *The Battles for Chattanooga: The Shipwreck of Their Hopes*. "The Kentuckians won."

Sergeants Harris H. Davis, Joseph Wagers and James Wood joined Wilson. So did Privates William Witt and Joseph Bradley. The six Kentuckians set off, scrambling up one hundred "feet or more of almost perpendicular wall, at a place where there was an irregular kind of a natural stairway, by which hung a large wild grape vine," the regimental history book noted.

Ogden said that ladders built for visitors also were available. "Lookout Mountain was a tourist attraction even before the Civil War," he explained. "The ladders were there to allow passage to the top for those who did not want to pay the toll to use the road. Some of the staged photos even show Wilson and his party climbing the ladders."

The Kentuckians beat the Pennsylvanians to the summit, from which the Confederates had indeed retreated. "Some fifteen or twenty minutes before sunrise, I unfurled the flag," the book quoted Wilson. He claimed it was "the highest flag planted during the war." (Soon afterward, the Pennsylvania soldiers displayed their regimental colors next to the Stars and Stripes, according to Cozzens.)

In any event, the sight of the American flag called "forth hearty cheers from below," recalled Wilson. He died in 1896 and is buried at Station Camp Cemetery, about four miles southwest of the marker.

The flag-raising scene is carved on one side of his tombstone, a four-sided obelisk. "It is one of the most interesting Civil War images I have ever seen," Ogden said. "It is folk art—Wilson standing with the flag on the tip of Lookout Mountain."

Meanwhile, later on November 25, 1863, the Yankees chased the Rebels off Missionary Ridge and won the Battle of Chattanooga. "Afterward, Captain Wilson and his men were photographed on Lookout Mountain with the battle flag," Ogden said. "At the time, the flag-raising was widely recognized as an important event."

The site is located in the Point Park section of the national military park close to the Adolph S. Ochs Observatory. "If you are standing at the observatory, it is right in front of you and below you. For safety reasons, it is blocked off. We don't want anybody to take one step too many."

Part III
1864–1865

"In View of Home, in the Midst of His Neighbors, He Laid Down His Life"

If he hadn't fallen in battle near his Paducah home, Colonel Albert P. Thompson might have been Paducah's second Confederate general.

"Had he lived longer, he would have received the commission of brigadier-general, a rank which had practically been his throughout most of his distinguished career," Henry George of Mayfield, an old Rebel comrade in arms, wrote of Thompson.

Paducahan Lloyd Tilghman did earn Confederate general's stars. He was mortally wounded in the Battle of Champion's Hill, near Vicksburg, Mississippi, on May 16, 1863.

Thompson perished in the Battle of Paducah on March 25, 1864. Reputedly, a Yankee cannonball took his head off. Thompson was thirty-five.

Before the war, Tilghman and Thompson were friends and fellow officers in the Paducah-based Southwest Battalion of the State Guard. In the summer of 1861, Tilghman led most of his men to Camp Boone, where they formed the nucleus of the Third Kentucky Infantry, a mainly Jackson Purchase outfit.

After Tilghman was promoted to general, Thompson took over as colonel of the Third Kentucky, which received its baptism of fire at Shiloh. Later in the war, the Third, Seventh and Eighth Kentucky Infantry Regiments were mounted and assigned to Forrest's cavalry. Forrest named Thompson commander of a brigade that included the Third, Seventh and Eighth Regiments plus the newly recruited Twelfth Kentucky Cavalry.

Thompson's brigade galloped into Paducah with Forrest and the rest of his raiders. Forrest split his force, leading some of his troopers to the waterfront while dispatching Thompson to Fort Anderson, an earth-walled strongpoint that the Yankees built to protect Paducah.

Forrest captured or destroyed large quantities of Union supplies and burned a steamboat. Thompson attacked Fort Anderson, which was supported by a pair of gunboats on the Ohio River.

Thompson met a grisly death, though some of the details are disputed. "He was instantly killed by the explosion of a shell," Major Henry George wrote in his book *A History of the 3rd, 7th, 8th and 12th Kentucky, C.S.A.* George soldiered in the Seventh Kentucky.

In his book *Paducahans in History*, Fred G. Neuman said, "Thompson was literally torn to pieces when a...32 [pound] cannon ball struck him while mounted on his favorite steed." According to *Center of Conflict*, "The cannonball decapitated Colonel Thompson, killed a horse ridden by Captain Al McGoodwin, and splattered nearby Confederate troops with blood."

Fort Anderson stood on the site of what became the Executive Inn hotel. According to Neuman, Thompson was killed "near the alley on Trimble street between Fifth and Sixth streets." There is a state historical marker in the general vicinity. Thompson lived at Seventh and Monroe Streets, Neuman wrote.

Having failed to capture the fort, Thompson was evidently plotting his next move when he was killed. It was dark, according to Neuman, and the colonel had gathered his staff officers for a parley.

Neuman said that the cannonball that claimed Thompson's life was fired from a gunboat. But Allen maintained that the fatal projectile was fired by Sergeant Tom Hayes of the Fifteenth Kentucky Cavalry who was part of a cannon crew. (The Battle of Paducah pitted western Kentuckian against western Kentuckian. Several of Fort Anderson's defenders, white and African American, were from the region.)

In addition, Neuman wrote that the cannonball also hit Thompson's horse, which "ran a half a block to Sixth Street and fell, and was later buried on the spot." Thompson is buried at the old Bowman Cemetery near Murray.

Thompson "had a compelling charm of manner and an earnestness and sincerity that won instant admiration and endeared him to his comrades in arms," Neuman wrote. "In view of home, in the midst of his neighbors, he laid down his life" was the epitaph carved on his tombstone.

"He Don't Put on So Much Style as Most Officers"

General John Buford's bravery at the Battle of Gettysburg was little noted nor long remembered in his native Kentucky.

"He is one of those all-but-forgotten heroes," said John Trowbridge. "But the Union army would never have won the battle without Buford's quick thinking and quick action on the first day."

Rebel infantry outnumbered and outgunned Buford's Yankee cavalry. Even so, the horsemen in blue stalled the Confederates long enough for General George G. Meade's Union Army of the Potomac to organize a defense and ultimately to win the Civil War's bloodiest battle, according to Trowbridge.

A bronze statue at Gettysburg National Military Park commemorates Buford's stand. "There are no monuments to John Buford in Kentucky that I know of," Trowbridge said.

Buford was born near Versailles, the Woodford County seat, in 1826. A state historical marker in town names Buford and five other county natives who were Civil War generals. "It is amazing that six could come from one small county," Trowbridge said.

Two generals named on the marker were Buford kin. His half brother, General Napoleon Bonaparte Buford, also fought for the Union. Their cousin, General Abraham Buford, donned Rebel gray.

John Buford moved with his parents to Rock Island, Illinois, in the 1840s. He graduated from West Point in 1848. The mustachioed, pipe-puffing Buford had little use for fancy uniforms and military spit and polish. "He don't put on so much style as most officers," one of his men said.

Though popular with his own troops, Buford was tough on the enemy. He hanged a Confederate guerrilla to a tree with a sign that warned, "This man to hang three days; he who cuts him down before shall hang the remaining time."

General John Buford. *Courtesy of the Library of Congress.*

The Buford Monument at Gettysburg. *Photo by the author.*

At Gettysburg, Buford's 2,700 horse soldiers were the first Union soldiers to make contact with General Robert E. Lee's Army of Northern Virginia. They galloped into town on the evening of June 30 in time to skirmish with some of Lee's advance units. Buford correctly figured that the whole Southern army would attack the next day.

On the morning of July 1, Buford deployed his men on high ground west of Gettysburg. More than seven thousand Rebels assaulted Buford's dismounted troopers around 9:00 a.m. "The two lines became hotly engaged, we having the advantage of position, he of numbers," the general reported.

His soldiers held on until General John F. Reynolds's infantry arrived around mid-morning. The blue-clad troops fell back through Gettysburg to higher ground, including Cemetery Ridge, where the Yankees stopped General George Pickett's historic charge on July 3 and won the battle.

Buford, who was badly wounded and left for dead after the 1862 Battle of Second Bull Run, Virginia, did not survive the Civil War. The general succumbed to typhoid fever on December 16, 1863, and was buried at West Point.

Buford, described by a Yankee colonel as "decidedly the best cavalry general" in the Army of the Potomac, was featured in *Gettysburg*, the 1994 movie and TV mini-series. Sam Elliott sported a Buford-style moustache in portraying the Kentucky general who, according to the colonel, could "always be relied on in any emergency."

"The Largest Training Camp for African Americans in Kentucky"

"I felt freedom in my bones," Sergeant Elijah Marrs remembered. "When I saw the American eagle with outspread wings, upon the [regimental]…flag, with the motto *E Pluribus Unum*, the thought came to me, 'Give me liberty or give me death.' Then all fear [was] banished."

Born in Shelby County, Marrs escaped bondage to fight for his freedom in the Civil War. He was one of more than ten thousand African Americans from Kentucky, almost all of them slaves, who were at Camp Nelson at one time or another. The site is a Jessamine County park.

Restored officers' quarters at Camp Nelson. *Photo by the author.*

Soldiers' families at Camp Nelson. *Courtesy of the University of Kentucky Archives.*

"This was the largest training camp for African Americans in Kentucky," said Mary Kozak, who helps supervise the park. "It was the third largest camp of its kind in the country."

Opened in 1863, Camp Nelson sprawled over 4,000 acres atop near-vertical cliffs that towered above the Kentucky River. Nearby, Hickman Creek snaked toward the river. Eight earthen forts added strength to the camp's natural defenses. The park preserves about 525 acres of the campsite, where the army drilled troops and stockpiled supplies for battles farther south.

The camp was named for General Nelson. White volunteers from the Bluegrass State and Tennessee learned soldiering at Camp Nelson before it welcomed black recruits in 1864. "The slaves became free when they enlisted," Kozak said. "Many of them brought their wives and children. There was no clear army policy as to what to do with them."

By July 1864, hundreds of army dependents were living in makeshift shelters in the camp. Camp commanders claimed that they were interfering with military operations. Numerous orders were issued to expel the refugees. The last, in November 1864, just as winter was coming on, proved deadly to many refugees.

To ensure that the soldiers' families would not return, the camp commander ordered the refugee huts burned. Left to fend for themselves outside the camp, hundreds of women and children perished from exposure or disease.

After the tragedy prompted angry protests in the North, the army allowed the survivors, many of them ill, back in the camp. "The army built duplex cottages for them under the direction of an officer and John G. Fee," Kozak said.

An antislavery Kentucky pastor, missionary and educator, Fee started Ariel College at Camp Nelson. He had founded integrated, coeducational Berea College in 1858.

Marrs had led twenty-seven other slaves to Louisville to enlist in the Union army. He joined the Twelfth United States Colored Heavy Artillery at Camp Nelson and earned sergeant's stripes. Also in 1864, Morgan raided nearby. Camp Nelson was down to only six hundred men, but he gave the post a wide berth, perhaps fearing it was too strongly fortified. "Every approach to the camp is commanded by mounted guns and so far as its natural defenses are concerned it is one of the most impregnable points in the country," said Captain Theron E. Hall, chief quartermaster at Camp Nelson.

The Twelfth Artillery saw combat elsewhere. The gunners helped defend Union positions against Confederate bands in central and western Kentucky.

After the war, Marrs taught school and became a Baptist minister. In 1879, he and his brother founded what became Simmons Bible College in Louisville.

Meanwhile, the army closed Camp Nelson in 1866. Two years later, Fee bought 130 acres of the site, including the refugee camp and adjoining farmland. He sold or leased the property back to the soldier families, according to an article by Dr. W. Stephen McBride featured on the Camp Nelson website www.campnelson.org.

At first, the refugee camp was named Ariel. Later, it became known as the Hall, a local meetinghouse, Kozak said.

Before it was disbanded, Camp Nelson grew to include about three hundred buildings, but only the officers' quarters remains. A commandeered 1850s-vintage farmhouse, the two-story, white painted wooden dwelling "has been meticulously restored to interpret it as a residence before and after the war and the officers' quarters during the war," Kozak said. The park also includes an interpretive center–museum.

The park, about six miles south of Nicholasville, the county seat, is open for guided tours Tuesdays through Saturdays from 10:00 a.m. to 5:00 p.m., local time.

Camp Nelson park also encompasses a rebuilt barracks and a restored Fort Putnam—one of the 1860s-vintage earthworks. In the park, too, are five miles of hiking trails with signs describing the camp. The trails are open from dawn to dusk.

"There are many unique historical sites in Jessamine County," said Kozak, the county's special projects director. "We are very dedicated to historic preservation in Jessamine County."

Kozak also said that Camp Nelson is a designated National Underground Network to Freedom and Lincoln Bicentennial site. Camp Nelson is off U.S. Highway 27 about a mile north of the Camp Nelson National Cemetery. The burial ground contains the graves of more than 9,500 veterans, including several Union soldiers who died at Camp Nelson or were killed in Civil War battles.

"THE DIFFERENCE BETWEEN A NAKED YANKEE AND A NAKED CONFEDERATE WOULD NOT BE NOTICED"

Sergeant Robert T. Pierce evidently looked like just another Rebel in need of a bath.

Stripped bare and lying, belly down, on a fence rail, he floated past several Southern soldiers washing themselves in Georgia's Chattahoochee River. "Good judgment told him that in the exhilaration of their sport, the difference between a naked Yankee and a naked Confederate would not be noticed," Tarrant wrote of his First Kentucky Cavalry comrade in arms.

Pierce was right. The Rebels didn't know that he was a Yankee on the lam again. This time, the Kentuckian got away for good, pulling off "one of the most adroit escapes from captivity" in the Civil War, according to *The Wild Riders.*

The Confederates had grabbed Pierce in eastern Tennessee in November 1863. After "several attempts" to flee his captors, he finally was able to give them the slip, Tarrant wrote. He added that the sergeant rejoined the First Kentucky shortly before the Rebels nabbed him again in July 1864. They seized him after the Battle of Moore's Bridge, a wooden span across the Chattahoochee not far from Atlanta.

The Rebels escorted him to General William Y.C. Humes. They questioned him for an hour, seeking information about the Union army. Pierce "was true and loyal to the core" and wouldn't talk, Tarrant wrote. But he offered Humes a novel proposition. "If the general would release him…on his return he would send a favorite Captain of theirs back in exchange," Tarrant wrote. If no swap could be arranged, Pierce said he would return to the Rebels.

Humes declined. "A Yankee's honor could not be risked so far," Tarrant explained. The Rebels put Pierce "under care of a strong guard, with strict orders to watch him closely," Tarrant wrote. He explained that First Kentucky Cavalry captives had "a reputation among the enemy of being hard to hold."

Tarrant added, "He was kept within fifty yards of the General's headquarters with the General's Staff, and escort around him. One guard was on duty all the time with a drawn pistol over him." The guard watched over Pierce as the prisoner lay down to sleep. But Pierce was only pretending. Just before sunup, the guard nodded off and Pierce slipped away.

"His captors had confiscated sixty dollars of his money, and also his boots, therefore he was in his 'sock feet,'" Tarrant wrote. "With cat-like tread…he moved off, glancing back to see if his action was noticed, till getting a safe distance, he advanced more briskly until he reached the thick woods.

Pierce decided not to make for the closest point to the river. Instead, he stole "through the undergrowth, now listening, his acute ears ever on the alert for voices and footsteps, now dodging, sometimes lying down in the weeds and bushes to keep from being seen by the passing enemy, about 10 o'clock he came near the river, a mile or two below the General's headquarters."

Pierce crept down a small creek "bordered with weeds and bushes" that flowed into the Chattahoochee. There, he spied the Rebel bathing party. "This would have alarmed most men in his situation, but not so with the cool-headed, self-possessed Sergeant; he saw a chance for his salvation," Tarrant wrote. He took off his uniform "of loyal blue." He tied his duds in a bundle and used his suspenders to sling the clothing below the handy rail he found nearby.

"Playing the role of one who could not swim without the rail, with his breast across the point where his clothes were fastened, he leisurely floated down through a gap among the bathers, until he reached beyond the main current of the swollen river, when he made for the opposite shore," Tarrant wrote. "Fortune favored him, for they seemed to pay no attention to his maneuvers. Hastily pulling his bundle from the rail, he ascended the river bank, in soft tones bidding his fellow-bathers 'good bye,' and swiftly made his way to a favorable spot where he donned his clothing."

Pierce reached the Union army "late in the evening" and regaled the troops, including General George Stoneman, with the story of his escape.

"It so happened that the captured Confederate Captain was present whom Pierce proposed to have exchanged for himself, and he lamented that Gen. Humes had not accepted his proposition for the exchange," Tarrant added.

Pierce enlisted on July 24, 1861. He was immediately made corporal of Company A, Tarrant's outfit.

"Shot by Order of the Federal Tyrant A.E. Paine on the Streets of Mayfield"

History barely records the fate of eighteen-year-old Henry Bascom Hicks, a schoolboy condemned as a Rebel spy and executed by a Yankee firing squad in Mayfield.

"He supposedly was shot into his grave after he refused to be blindfolded and told the soldiers, 'I can look you in the eye,'" said Barton, who added that Hicks was an unsung local hero who deserves more from posterity.

Shot in 1864, Hicks was buried at Mayfield's old Maplewood Cemetery. A four-foot marble shaft marks his grave, which is also covered by a newer stone slab. The Confederate Veterans Association of Graves County put up the shaft in 1892. Tilghman-Beauregard Camp No. 1460, Sons of Confederate Veterans, had the slab placed in 1990.

The slab repeats a barely legible inscription on the weatherworn, lichen-encrusted shaft that charges that young Hicks was "shot by order of the Federal tyrant A.E. Paine on the streets of Mayfield, Kentucky." The inscription backs up Barton's claim that Hicks spurned a blindfold and defiantly declared to his executioners, "I can look you in the eye."

The grave of Henry Bascom Hicks. *Photo by the author.*

The monument gave the "Federal tyrant" the wrong initials. He was General E.A. Paine of Ohio, who took command of strongly pro-Confederate western Kentucky in 1864. To local Rebel sympathizers, the bluecoat officer was a close encounter of the worst kind; "Gen. Pain," they dubbed him.

Before Union authorities removed him, Paine was guilty of a fifty-one-day "reign of violence, terror, extortion, oppression, bribery and military murders," according to Lewis and Richard Collins's *History of Kentucky*.

The book is not unsympathetic to the "Lost Cause." But Paine's reputation doesn't fare much better among modern Kentucky historians, such as Harrison and Klotter. "Paine raised a hundred thousand dollars from a special tax to benefit the families of Union soldiers; that money disappeared," they wrote in *A New History of Kentucky*. "Prominent citizens suspected of Confederate sympathies were fined or exiled or both—unless they could purchase an exemption from the charges."

What's more, Harrison and Klotter added, "a 25 percent tax was placed on cotton that had had contact with anyone suspected of being pro-Confederate, and a tax was levied on the mail of Union soldiers." They also wrote that "several persons were executed on Paine's orders without even a pretense of trial." While Harrison and Klotter cited the case of Hicks, apparently no other history book tells about him.

"Hicks wasn't in the army, but his brothers were," Barton said. "I guess it was a case of guilt by association."

In any event, some Union soldiers arrested Hicks in Mayfield on August 21, 1864, and marched him to Yankee headquarters at the Graves County Courthouse. Reputedly, it was lunchtime. "The commander of the post, one of Paine's subordinates, is supposed to have told Hicks, 'We have no vittles for a man such as you,'" Barton said.

After being judged a Confederate spy, Hicks was ordered to be shot at 2:00 p.m. Rifle-armed soldiers led the teenager away and executed him. "Folklore says the Yankees made him dig his own grave," Barton said. "He may have been reburied in the cemetery."

Barton said that Hicks's story deserves more publicity. Maplewood is famous for the Wooldridge Monuments, an unmoving procession of stone statuary, including people and animals, that memorializes a well-to-do man named Henry Wooldridge. A state historical marker explains the monuments, which were heavily damaged in a 2009 ice storm. But the account of Hicks's death is almost unknown, Barton said. "And that's a shame," he added. "This young man was a genuine hero."

Paine wasn't, according to *Generals in Blue*, by Ezra J. Warner. The book includes brief biographies of all the Union generals. Paine's military career, none too distinguished anyway, went downhill after his western Kentucky stint, according to Warner. "Thereafter he was 'awaiting orders' until he finally submitted his resignation, which was accepted to date from April 5, 1865," Warner wrote.

Paine's final resting place is less heralded than Hicks's grave. After the war, Paine ended up in Jersey City, New Jersey, where he died in 1882. His grave at a church cemetery is unmarked; the cemetery records have disappeared, and hence the exact location is unknown, according to Warner.

"What an Insignificant Little Cuss I Surrendered To"

Hopkinsville had a real *High Noon* moment.

"But unlike in the cowboy movie, we helped our law officer," said Donna Stone, director of the Pennyroyal Area Museum. The museum is close to where Officer Paul Fuller, backed by several armed men, slew Rebel raider Thomas G. Woodward and frightened away his band. "The story is pretty well known in Hopkinsville," Stone said.

In *High Noon*, the murderous Miller gang is expected to hit Hadleyville on the noon train. The citizens skedaddle, leaving Sheriff Will Kane, played by Gary Cooper, to face the bad guys solo on the silver screen.

Fuller had ample assistance when Colonel Woodward, who lived near Hopkinsville, rode into town during the Civil War. The August 19, 1864 showdown happened near Ninth and Main Streets in the Christian County seat.

Woodward was known as a daring cavalry commander. Reminiscent of "Stovepipe" Johnson, he crafted a pair of "cannons" out of logs and bluffed a Yankee colonel into giving up Clarksville, Tennessee, without a fight in 1862. The Union officer allegedly got Woodward to pose for a photograph so he could show his friends up north "what an insignificant little cuss I surrendered to."

By 1864, Woodward was out of favor with the Confederate brass. The young colonel had been disciplined "and deprived of his command," according to *A History of Christian County Kentucky from Oxcart to Airplane* by Charles M. Meacham.

Undaunted, Woodward gathered a few horsemen and boasted that he was going to seize Hopkinsville. The mostly pro-Union town was defended by Union troops and Home Guards, including Officer Fuller.

At the edge of Hopkinsville, all but one of Woodward's men forsook their leader, who was drunk, according to Meacham. The soldier who stuck with Woodward "endeavored to dissuade him from the foolhardy undertaking, as the windows along Main Street were filled with armed men."

Finally, Woodward's companion turned back, leaving the colonel to ride on alone. When Woodward was almost to Ninth and Main Streets, he aimed his pistol at a window manned by Peyton Breathitt, evidently an ancestor of Governor Edward T. Breathitt of Hopkinsville. Before Woodward could squeeze the trigger, shots rang out from several windows. A quintet of bullets struck Woodward and his steed; man and beast slumped to the street. Hearing the distant shooting, Woodward's men fired a parting volley down Main Street and galloped away.

Meanwhile, Woodward was carried to a hotel, where he died in a few minutes, according to Meacham. The colonel was buried at old Riverside Cemetery.

"Paul Fuller claimed the credit of killing him," Meacham wrote. "The Home Guards did not dispute his claim."

There is nothing at Ninth and Main to commemorate the bloody shootout. But a bullet-scarred sugar maple survived into the twentieth century, Meacham wrote.

Fuller himself died close to where Woodward was gunned down. A few years later, the officer "became involved in a shooting affray almost on the spot…and was himself shot to death," Meacham wrote.

CIVIL WAR HERO IS BURIED UNSUNG AT LEBANON JUNCTION

There are no memorials to Civil War hero Henry B. Mattingly in Marion County, where he was born, or in Bullitt County, where he is buried.

"When I was growing up in Bullitt County, I was totally unaware of him or the fact that he was a Medal of Honor recipient," confessed author and historian Dennis W. Belcher. Most Medal of Honor winners rate special military tombstones. A simple civilian stone marks Mattingly's grave.

The gray slab notes nothing about the Medal of Honor. Nor does it say that Mattingly earned his country's highest military decoration for "exceptionally heroic and meritorious conduct" at the Battle of Jonesboro, Georgia, on September 1, 1864.

Mattingly captured the battle flag of the consolidated Sixth and Seventh Arkansas Infantry Regiments. "Many men died defending their regimental colors in the Civil War," Belcher said. "They were symbols of personal, state and national pride. To lose one's colors was to lose one's honor."

Belcher, who lives in Columbia, Missouri, wrote *The Tenth Kentucky Volunteer Infantry in the Civil War: A History and Roster*. Mattingly was a private in the regiment, which Belcher says "was composed of men primarily from Marion and Washington counties."

Raised in November 1861 for three years' service, the Tenth Kentucky fought in several battles in the western theatre. "They included the battles of Chickamauga and Missionary Ridge," Belcher said. "The regiment also fought in the Atlanta campaign, its service culminating in the battle of Jonesboro."

Born in 1844, Mattingly was seventeen years old when he signed up with the regiment in 1861. "He was a farmer," Belcher said. He was a veteran soldier when he fought in the Battle of Jonesboro, a Union victory that led to the fall of nearby Atlanta. The Tenth Kentucky served under General William T. Sherman, whose army had been besieging the city.

By the end of August, the hard-pressed Confederates were down to their last rail supply line, which ran through Jonesboro, Belcher said. Sherman sent most of his army, including the Tenth Kentucky, to Jonesboro to seize the tracks. "The Confederates were equally determined not to let their supply line be severed," Belcher explained.

The Rebels attacked on August 31 but were repulsed and forced to retreat to their earthworks. Sherman counterattacked the next day, shoving the Rebels back. "Once the Confederate line was broken, some of the fiercest fighting of the war ensued," Belcher said. "Fighting was vicious and hand to hand." Badly beaten, the Confederate army abandoned Atlanta on the night of September 1. Sherman's army marched into the city the next day.

Meanwhile, soldiers of the Tenth Kentucky had been among the first Union troops to breach the enemy's works at Jonesboro. "The amputated arms and limbs and torn bodies of the wounded officers... speak more eloquently than any poor words of mine can do [of] their noble conduct," reported the commander of the brigade that included the Tenth Kentucky.

Colonel William H. Hayes, the Tenth Kentucky commander, praised Mattingly in his official report. "The enemy immediately in our front was the Sixth and Seventh Arkansas Regiments, of Cleburne's division, consolidated. We captured their flag, which has been sent to brigade headquarters. Private Henry B. Mattingly...had the honor of capturing these colors."

Mattingly was rewarded with the Medal of Honor on April 7, 1865. The citation noted that he displayed "exceptionally heroic and meritorious conduct" by capturing the enemy colors.

Jonesboro was the Tenth Kentucky's last battle. The regiment was disbanded in November 1864, and the men went home or joined other regiments.

Apparently, few outfits shed more blood for the Union cause than the Tenth Kentucky. About 221 of the 950 men who soldiered in the regiment perished in combat or died of battle wounds or disease. Others were captured.

"The regiment was down to 152 men at Jonesboro," Belcher said.

Mattingly was lucky. He survived the war evidently without serious injury and returned to Marion County. He married Amanda Tucker of Loretto in 1868; the couple had two sons and a daughter. Henry moved his family to

Shepherdsville, the Bullitt County seat, and lived there until he died in either 1892 or 1893, records show. His tombstone reads 1893.

Records also show that he was buried in a family cemetery at Pitts Point in Bullitt County. His remains and what appears to be the original tombstone were removed to the Lebanon Junction Cemetery in 1966. A newer bronze footstone only identifies him as "PVT CO. B 10 KY INF CIVIL WAR."

"YOU CAN DO ANYTHING ELSE YOU WANT TO KENTUCKIANS, JUST DON'T MESS WITH THEIR HOGS"

The scandal went down in Kentucky history as the "Great Hog Swindle."

It purportedly cost Bluegrass State pig farmers at least $300,000 during the Civil War. The "scurvy" scheme, according to E. Merton Coulter, was "the most brazen attempt of the military authorities to enrich themselves at the expense of the Kentucky people."

Writing in *The Civil War and Readjustment in Kentucky*, Coulter added that the hog swindle was "the lowest and meanest prostitution of the power to regulate trade."

The supposed ringleader was Georgetown-born General Stephen G. Burbridge, Union military commander in his native state. On October 28, 1864, he issued a proclamation asking farmers to sell their "surplus" swine to the government.

Louisville-based Major Henry C. Symonds, a supply officer, sold Burbridge on the "hog order," according to *The Civil War in Kentucky* by Lowell H. Harrison. Symonds claimed that he could save the government money "by buying hogs directly from Kentucky farmers and packing the pork for the army without going through the usual contractors."

Speculators had pushed pork prices way up. Convinced that they and certain meatpackers were in cahoots against him, Symonds illegally awarded contracts to other packers who agreed to cooperate with him, according to Harrison.

Burbridge's order promised farmers "a fair market price" for their swine. Government purchasing agents "offered nevertheless from one to two cents a pound less than the Cincinnati and Louisville market," Coulter wrote.

To ensure plenty of porkers for the army, Burbridge forbade shipment of pigs outside Kentucky without a permit, Harrison wrote. Soldiers in

General Stephen
G. Burbridge.
Courtesy of the
Library of Congress.

Covington and Newport were to arrest farmers who tried to sell hogs in Cincinnati and confiscate their swine.

Governor Thomas E. Bramlette complained to Lincoln that Burbridge's hog order had produced "considerable commotion" among Bluegrass State farmers and packers. He urged Lincoln to make Burbridge repeal the hog order. Lincoln did, but not until after the presidential election.

Lincoln did not stand a chance to carry Kentucky. Nonetheless, historians say that the Great Hog Swindle probably cost Lincoln some votes in his native state. The president won another term but again lost Kentucky in a landslide.

By the time Burbridge cancelled the hog order on November 27, 1864, Bramlette estimated that "farmers had sustained losses to at least $300,000." The governor added that losses could have gone "over one million dollars."

In February 1865, Burbridge was removed from command in Kentucky. Neither he nor Symonds was charged with trying to line his own pockets by cheating hog farmers.

Historians agree that the Great Hog Swindle further strained relations between Kentucky, a loyal border state, and the White House. Klotter wrote in *The Kentucky Encyclopedia* that "the so-called great hog swindle…turned even loyal Kentuckians against the administration and [made them] pro-Southern."

Duane Bolin, a Murray State University history professor and author, sees another side to the scandal. "It proved that you can do anything else you want to Kentuckians, just don't mess with their hogs."

"THERE'S JUST WHISKEY ENOUGH FOR THE GENERAL"

Confederate Captain Frank Gracey didn't ride to glory in the Civil War. He swam, naked, in October.

Using a log or a plank for a float, the Eddyville Rebel crossed the chilly Tennessee River near New Concord and single-handedly captured the *Mazeppa*, a Yankee steamboat. "It was one of the most amazing feats of the Civil War," said historian and museum consultant Jerry Wooten of Nashville.

Gracey was with Forrest when he sneaked his cavalry army into abandoned Fort Heiman. "Forrest used his cannons to shell boats on the river," said Wooten, who earned a master's degree in history at Murray State University. "He even captured two boats and used them against the Yankees for a while."

The *Mazeppa* was Forrest's first victim. After his horse soldiers leisurely looted the boat, they burned and sank it. The boat's remains are apparently still in Kentucky Lake, which the construction of Kentucky Dam created in the 1940s. Fort Heiman is on private property; the lake also flooded the site of Fort Henry, which was opposite Fort Heiman.

After Forrest took over the fort, his artillerymen made short work of a handful of unsuspecting Union river craft, starting with the *Mazeppa*, a supply boat. Rebel gunners crippled the steamer, but it ran aground across the Tennessee from Fort Heiman.

Forrest's troopers had hoped to help themselves to the *Mazeppa*'s cargo, but they had no boat to cross the river. Gracey, an officer in the Third Kentucky

Mounted Infantry, volunteered to go skinny-dipping for the *Mazeppa*. "He stripped himself bare, slung two great hoss pistols around his neck" and paddled over "belly down like a frog" on the log or plank, Allen wrote in *Center of Conflict*.

Frank Gracey caught the boat's frightened crew hiding in a canebrake. "He got the drop on them with his hoss pistols and the crew meekly surrendered to a naked giant, his body still glistening from the river," Allen wrote.

Gracey returned to the fort in a skiff he commandeered from the *Mazeppa*. He brought a rope to his comrades in arms, who pulled the steamboat over "like…leading a mule back on the farm," Allen wrote. Gracey also rowed back with General Abe Buford, a Forrest subordinate, "so that the surrender of the crew and boat could be made in proper style," Allen wrote.

As the *Mazeppa* neared Fort Heiman, the soldiers saw Buford standing on the deck and swigging from a whiskey jug. They begged him not to drink it all.

According to Allen, Buford replied, "Take it easy boys. There's plenty of meat, plenty of hardtack and plenty of clothes here for all you boys. But there's just whiskey enough for the general."

"You Are Just the Man I Wanted to See"

Rebel Captain Frank Gracey wasn't the only Kentuckian to swim to glory in the Civil War.

Yankee Major John Francis Weston did likewise, but in Alabama. He won the Medal of Honor to boot.

"This officer, with a small detachment, while en route to destroy steamboats loaded with supplies for the enemy, was stopped by an unfordable river, but with 5 of his men [the *New York Times* reported it was 6] swam the river, captured 2 leaky canoes, and ferried his men across," Weston's Medal of Honor citation reads. "He then encountered and defeated the enemy, and on reaching Wetumpka found the steamers [only one, according to the *Times*] anchored in midstream. By a ruse obtained possession of a boat, with which he reached the steamers and demanded and received their surrender."

The date was April 13, 1865.

Weston, a Louisville native who served in the Fourth Kentucky Cavalry, stayed in the army long after the Civil War. He made general, died at age sixty and was buried in Arlington National Cemetery.

Weston was barely sixteen years old when he was commissioned a first lieutenant in the Fourth Kentucky in November 1861. The regiment was organized in his hometown. Weston made major in November 1864, six months before he bloodlessly bagged the Rebel supply boat—or boats—close to Wetumpka. He and his troopers didn't have to fire a shot.

In the spring of 1865 (the *Times* erroneously reported that it was "the summer of 1864"), the Fourth Kentucky was attached to General James H. Wilson's cavalry army. On April 13, the regiment was about forty miles from Montgomery, the Alabama capital, when Weston heard that "there was a Confederate transport laden with supplies somewhere near the junction of the Tallapoosa and Coosa Rivers," the *Times* reported in a 1905 story headlined "America's Badge of Bravery: What It Means." Weston got orders to find the enemy vessel and seize it.

When he and his horse soldiers reached the Tallapoosa, Weston "saw on the further side of the river two or three canoes which he thought might be useful to him in hunting the transport," the story added. "Strapping his revolver on the top of his head, and ordering his men to do likewise, the Major, with six followers, plunged into the river, swam to the opposite bank and secured the canoes."

Weston rowed back to bring the rest of his soldiers across. Leaving a handful of men to guard the horses, Weston led his troopers upriver in the captured canoes. "At the mouth of the Coosa he discovered the transport in a bayou a short distance ahead," the *Times* noted.

"Beaching his canoes he began to make signals to attract the attention of those on board the transport, and presently saw a gig push off and pull toward shore," the story explained. "When the gig ran upon the beach the first man to step out of it was the Captain of the transport."

The captain was curious. "What do you want with me?" he asked the major, according to the *Times*. "Who may you be?" Weston replied.

"I am the Captain of the boat out there," the skipper said.

Weston, the newspaper reported, told the captain, "Then you are just the man I wanted to see. I command the advance of Wilson's cavalry, which will be along here in a few minutes, and must ask you to surrender yourself and your transport."

The captain, "after a moment's thought," capitulated unconditionally to the Kentucky cavalry commander, the *Times* noted. Weston and a few of his soldiers boarded the gig and rowed to the transport. Weston told the officer in charge that the boat's captain had given up "and that he had come to take possession of the boat."

The crew complied. "The transport was promptly turned over, taken to Montgomery and destroyed," the *Times* reported.

Weston didn't receive his Medal of Honor until 1898. By then he was a brigadier general.

"EXTRAORDINARY VALOR IN THE FACE OF DEADLY ENEMY FIRE"

Andrew Jackson Smith saw the color-bearer die with Old Glory in his grasp.

A Kentuckian who escaped slavery to fight for his freedom, Smith grabbed the battle flag. Waving the Stars and Stripes over his head, the twenty-one-year-old Union soldier helped rally his comrades against the Rebel foe.

Smith's bravery in the Civil War earned him the Congressional Medal of Honor, but not until 2001, more than 136 years after his feat of "extraordinary valor in the face of deadly enemy fire." Seventeen African Americans won the Medal of Honor in the Civil War. Smith was the only one from the Bluegrass State.

A Kentucky Historical Society marker in the Land Between The Lakes near Grand Rivers tells the story of "this Medal of Honor recipient…born a slave in Lyon County, Ky., on September 3, 1843." Smith, who died in nearby Grand Rivers at age eighty-eight, is buried in Mount Pleasant Cemetery on the hilltop above the marker.

Between the Rivers Incorporated got the marker erected next to the Trace, the main LBL highway. The local nonprofit group also helped arrange a special Medal of Honor tombstone for the old soldier, whose grave is shaded by ramrod-straight oak and cedar trees.

A small American flag is stuck in the sandy soil next to the gray granite military headstone. "MEDAL OF HONOR" and a gold-painted, star-shaped outline of the coveted decoration are chiseled into the grave marker, which is a regulation thirty-nine inches tall, one foot wide and four inches thick.

Ray Parish, Between the Rivers president, got the stone through the Veterans' Administration. "They told me how to proceed and what documentation to provide," he said. "The VA approved the marker, shipped it to me and we put it up in the cemetery."

A surgeon who served with Smith nominated him for the Medal of Honor in 1916. The army rejected the nomination, citing lack of evidence.

Left: Andrew Jackson Smith. *Courtesy of the Library of Congress.*

Below: Smith Highway. *Photo by the author.*

ANDREW JACKSON SMITH

This Medal of Honor recipient was born a slave in Lyon County, Ky., on September 3, 1843. Andrew Jackson Smith escaped to Union Army at 19 and fell in with 41st Illinois. Wounded at Battle of Shiloh. Recuperated at Clinton, Illinois, where he heard that blacks could join the Union Army. He mustered in Co. B, 55th Mass. Colored Infantry, May 16, 1863.

Racism was likely a factor, too, according to the office of U.S. Senator Dick Durbin, an Illinois Democrat. Durbin and now retired Republican U.S. Representative Tom Ewing, also from Illinois, campaigned for congressional approval of the Medal of Honor for Smith. Durbin called the belated award "a wrong righted."

The Smith grave and the Medal of Honor tombstone. *Photo by the author.*

Early in the Civil War, Smith and another slave decided to enlist in the Union army after they learned that their masters planned to join the Confederates and take them along. The closest Federal troops were at Smithland, twenty-five miles from where Smith and the other slave lived. Undaunted, they fled at night through mostly pro-Confederate countryside. Icy rain made the journey more perilous.

Fearful of being mistaken for Rebels and shot, the half-frozen Smith and his companion waited until daylight to approach the Yankees. The Union troops welcomed the weary wayfarers, providing them food, dry clothes and shelter.

Neither slave was permitted to enlist. Smith volunteered as a servant to Major John Warner of the Forty-first Illinois Infantry. Smith agreed to return Warner's belongings to Clinton, Illinois, the major's home, should the officer be killed.

Smith was with Warner at the Battle of Fort Donelson. At the Battle of Shiloh, the Rebels shot two horses from under Warner. Unhurt, the officer rode back into combat astride a Confederate horse that Smith managed to capture.

Minutes later, Smith suffered a head wound that almost killed him. A spent rifle bullet struck him in the left temple and ended up lodged in his forehead, between skin and bone. After the slug was removed at a field hospital, Smith recuperated in Warner's hometown, where he heard about the Emancipation Proclamation.

In 1863, Smith traveled to Boston and mustered into the Fifty-fifth Massachusetts Colored Infantry, a sister regiment of the storied Fifty-fourth Massachusetts, which was featured in the popular movie *Glory*. "Corporal Smith ended up fighting over on the Georgia and South Carolina coasts," Parish said.

The Fifty-fourth and Fifty-fifth Regiments were part of a Union force that attacked the Confederates at Honey Hill, South Carolina, on November 30, 1864. Rebel fire killed and wounded "half of the officers and a third of the enlisted men" in Smith's five-hundred-man regiment, his Medal of Honor citation explains.

When shrapnel claimed the life of the corporal carrying the Fifty-fifth's battle flag, Smith "took the Regimental Colors…through heavy [artillery]… fire," the citation adds.

> *Corporal Smith continued to expose himself to enemy fire by carrying the colors throughout the battle. Through his actions, the Regimental Colors of the 55th Infantry Regiment were not lost to the enemy. Corporal Andrew Jackson Smith's extraordinary valor in the face of deadly enemy fire is in keeping with the highest traditions of military service and reflects great credit upon him, the 55th Regiment, and the United States Army.*

Smith didn't rescue just the Stars and Stripes. Later, he saved the blue Fifty-fifth Massachusetts regimental flag when the sergeant carrying it was wounded. After the battle, Smith was promoted to sergeant for preserving the two flags.

Following the Civil War, Smith bought land in Lyon County near Grand Rivers, a Livingston County community, and became a prosperous citizen, Parish said. Smith lived his last years in Grand Rivers, now a Kentucky Lake resort.

Andrew S. Bowman of Indianapolis, Smith's grandson, was determined that his forebear would receive the Medal of Honor. He spent several years collecting records, conducting research and working with Durbin and other government officials and a history professor at Illinois State University.

Bowman received the medal on behalf of his grandfather from President Bill Clinton in a White House ceremony in early 2001. Also present was Caruth Smith-Washington of Las Vegas, A.J. Smith's daughter and Bowman's aunt.

Bowman's grandfather is memorialized by more than a marker and a special tombstone in western Kentucky. "We got two miles of Kentucky 453 officially named the 'Andrew Jackson Smith Memorial Highway,'" Parish said. The stretch of two-lane blacktop is just north of LBL, where the highway becomes the Trace.

"It Was a Horrible Butchery"

The "Simpsonville Slaughter" is not in most history books.

However, a state historical society marker a half-mile west of the Shelby County town tells where Confederate guerrillas "with feelings of delight" massacred African American soldiers on January 25, 1865.

The marker is on U.S. Highway 60. John Trowbridge helped get it erected at the site of the atrocity.

"For a long time, the massacre was largely unknown," he said. "But it was reported in many newspapers in Kentucky and other states. It was called the 'Simpsonville Slaughter.'"

The mass killings outraged the *Louisville Journal*. "It is presumed that the Negroes surrendered and were shot down in cold blood, as but two of the entire number escaped," the paper reported.

The slain soldiers were members of Company E, Fifth United States Colored Cavalry. Guerrillas surprised the troopers just after they left Simpsonville. The Union soldiers were herding about nine hundred head of cattle to Louisville from their base at Camp Nelson, Trowbridge said.

The marker notes that the guerrillas killed about twenty-two troopers and wounded eight more. "But the numbers vary, depending on the source," Trowbridge said.

The *Journal* claimed the guerrillas killed thirty-five troopers. "It was a horrible butchery, yet the scoundrels engaged in the bloody work shot down their victims with feelings of delight," the newspaper noted.

Henry Magruder, a notorious Kentucky bushwhacker, took credit for the massacre. He claimed that fifteen other guerrillas were with him, including the infamous William Clark Quantrill and Marcellus Jerome Clark, alias "Sue Mundy."

Federal authorities hanged Magruder and Clark for their many bloody misdeeds. Union troops wounded and captured Quantrill, a Missourian who crossed into Kentucky late in the war. The outlaw died before he could be executed.

Before they killed the black troops, the guerrillas raided Simpsonville and stole about $1,200, according to the *Journal*. Minutes before, the soldiers had resumed the cattle drive without their officers, who were white. They were "loafing in the tavern" but managed to elude the guerrillas, the paper reported.

"In about half an hour the guerrillas returned; loaded down with booty, and stated that they had killed twenty-five of the Negroes," the *Journal* also reported. The paper described the massacre site as "a terrible scene. The ground was stained with blood and the dead bodies of Negro soldiers were stretched out along the road."

The *Journal* also condemned the absent white officers. "It is certain that if they had been with their men, and enforced a proper discipline, the outlaws would have been whipped with ease." Trowbridge said that no Union officer was held responsible or accountable for the massacre.

Meanwhile, the *Journal* praised local citizens "without distinction of party" for helping tend the wounded and bury the dead in a common roadside grave. The burial ground became an African American cemetery, but it was abandoned about 1965 and all but forgotten, Trowbridge said.

The marker also notes that the Fifth Cavalry fought in the Battle of Saltville, Virginia, in October 1864. Afterward, some of the victorious Confederates slaughtered a number of wounded Union soldiers, most of them Fifth Cavalry troopers, in what became known as "the Saltville Massacre."

"At the House of a Deserter…We Learned that President Davis Had Been Captured"

When the Yankees captured Christian County–born Jefferson Davis, Hazard Perry Baker of adjoining Trigg County offered his sword as a token of surrender.

Baker, a Rebel lieutenant, doesn't even rate a line in most history books. Neither do Captain Given Campbell and the other Trigg cavalrymen who rode as the Confederate president's personal escort when he tried to escape Union troops after the Civil War.

Baker's story was told on a state historical marker on U.S. Highway 68 in Canton, a tiny Trigg County community on Lake Barkley. The officer is buried in a cemetery four miles south of the metal plaque.

Campbell carried a diary titled "Memorandum of a Journal, Kept Daily during the last March of Jefferson Davis." Owned by the Library of

Congress, the record describes the flight of Davis through the Carolinas to southern Georgia, where Union cavalry caught him on May 10, 1865.

Campbell and his men were part of a small cavalry force that rendezvoused with the Davis party at Greensboro, North Carolina. In the presidential entourage was another famous Kentuckian, General John C. Breckinridge, Confederate secretary of war. Campbell said that Davis "appeared well on horseback," thin but not "frail or weak."

In South Carolina, Davis chose Campbell and his men as a personal escort. Traveling on, the little caravan of wagons and horsemen reached Washington, Georgia, where more than $200,000 in money and gold from the Rebel treasury were left with still-loyal Confederates. To speed his escape, Davis pared down his escort.

He asked Campbell to choose "a few faithful hearts who would be willing to go as [Davis's] escort." After the captain named Baker and seven other men, the president gave Campbell "a pair of large revolvers, Kerr's Patent." At Abbeville, Georgia, Davis spent the night in his tent with his wife, Varina, who had been traveling with their children in a separate caravan. Two of Campbell's scouts, "their horses showing the effects of…hard and rapid ride," reported that four hundred Union troopers were close.

The presidential train moved cautiously up the road toward Irwinville and then stopped on the morning of May 9. Alarmed, Campbell said he "took the liberty of suggesting to President Davis the danger of this delay and the readiness with which the enemy's cavalry could pursue so broad a train."

Yankee horsemen were not Davis's only worry, Campbell recorded. Davis "seemed very much impressed for the safety of his wife and children, on account of the large number of deserters from the Confederate Army residing in the adjacent counties." Davis ordered Campbell to take a man and find a place to cross a river near Irwinville.

Campbell "remonstrated against leaving the president at that time and suggested that he send another party." Nonetheless, Campbell rode ahead. On May 10, he made the last entry in his diary: "At the house of a deserter…we learned that President Davis had been captured that morning, North of and near Irwinville."

In Campbell's absence, Baker was in command of Davis's escort. When he offered his sword to the leader of the Yankee troops who captured Davis, the Union officer gallantly returned it. Campbell, Baker and the Trigg County troopers in gray made it home after the war. Baker's sword ended up with Arthur C. Burnett of Cadiz, who donated it to the United Daughters of the Confederacy.

Part IV

More Tales, Monumental and Otherwise

"They Fought as Bravely as Any Troops in the Fort"

Kentucky furnished more African American troops to the Union army than any other state except Louisiana. Yet only one memorial—in Frankfort, the Kentucky capital—was erected to Bluegrass State black volunteers.

"In Memory of the Colored Soldiers Franklin County, Kentucky Who Fought in the Civil War" is chiseled on the base of the gray stone shaft at Green Hill Cemetery, a traditionally African American burial ground. The names of 142 soldiers are carved into the stone. (Frankfort is also the seat of Franklin County.)

Reportedly, the Frankfort monument is one of only four memorials to black Union veterans in the country. They were officially designated "United States Colored Troops."

In Kentucky, African Americans were not recruited for the Union forces until 1863. Even so, the state was credited with 23,703 black soldiers.

Almost all Kentucky whites—even the most ardent Unionists—fiercely opposed the enlistment of African Americans. After the war, Kentucky became part of the Jim Crow South, where segregation and racial discrimination were the law and the social order.

"No public official in Kentucky endorsed the idea [of recruiting black troops], and most private citizens were bitter in their denunciation of the

The Colored Soldiers Monument. *Courtesy of the Library of Congress.*

proposal," Harrison wrote in *The Civil War in Kentucky.*

Nearly all Kentucky whites believed that their skin color alone made them superior to African Americans. "The idea that a black could become a combat soldier challenged the concept of black inferiority that was at the heart of any defense of slavery," Harrison added.

Similarly, Coulter wrote in *The Civil War and Readjustment in Kentucky* that "it was past comprehension of [white] Kentuckians" that anybody could favor turning "a slave into a soldier, a rank of distinction held particularly high in the traditions of the state."

Coulter cited a state representative who "arose in Frankfort and declared that Lincoln was a usurper and a tyrant and that he would never allow his son to fight beside a negro soldier." He also quoted Governor Bramlette, who said that making a soldier out of a black man "humiliates the just pride of loyal men." Bramlette added that after the war black veterans could "never remain and live amongst those against whom they have been in battle array."

Nonetheless, African American units were formed across Kentucky from Maysville to Paducah, notes a cemetery sign that describes the Frankfort monument. Most of the black troops joined up at Camp Nelson and at Columbus.

Organized at Columbus in June 1863, the Fourth U.S. Colored Field Artillery (Heavy) was Kentucky's first African American outfit. "The last to organize was the 128th U.S. Colored Infantry, February 12–June 2, 1865 at Louisville," the sign adds.

A sign at Columbus-Belmont State Park, which encompasses Confederate fortifications occupied by Union forces in 1862, also describes the Fourth Heavy Artillery. "The Fourth was largely recruited in the Columbus area," the sign reads. "Because of opposition by Kentucky's political leaders the enlistments of African Americans in the Army, no such units have a Kentucky designation," the Columbus sign notes.

All told, Kentucky furnished twenty-three African American regiments—two cavalry, four field artillery (heavy) and seventeen infantry. "Kentucky African American soldiers initially were assigned to guard and garrison duty around the Commonwealth at Camp Nelson, Louisville, Crab Orchard, Danville, Camp Wildcat, Smithland and Louisa," the sign reads.

Black troops battled guerrillas at Lexington, Harrodsburg, Haddix's Ferry, Owensboro and Ghent, according to the sign. But they also served outside the state.

In addition, the First—later the Eighth—U.S. Colored Artillery (Heavy) helped defend Paducah's Fort Anderson against Forrest. Most of the Union troops—including the African American artillerymen—had never been under fire, according to Colonel Stephen G. Hicks, Fort Anderson's commander.

"And here permit me to remark that I have never been one of those men who ever had much confidence in colored troops fighting, but those doubts are now all removed, for they fought as bravely as any troops in the fort," Hicks said in his official battle report.

Similar remarks from a white officer—Thomas Speed of Kentucky—are printed on the sign in Green Hill Cemetery. Speed witnessed Kentucky African Americans assault Fort Fisher, North Carolina, on February 25, 1865. "You must not turn up your nose when I say they fight splendidly," he wrote his wife. "I saw them tried yesterday. And our regiment saw it and they all acknowledged that we have to give it up…[these men] will fight."

The sign also quotes the *Frankfort State Journal* of July 3, 1924: "The monument has been erected at a cost of several hundred dollars under the direction of the Colored Women's Relief Corps, and each soldier's name has been cut in the stone. Contributions are being made to the fund by patriotic and public spirited citizens of both races."

Kuttawa Monument Memorializes Famous Confederate Cannoneers

It might be the most forlorn of Kentucky's Confederate monuments. "Cobb's Battery" is molded into the concrete base of the pointy, six-foot

The Cobb's Battery Monument. *Photo by the author.*

stone memorial next to Lake Barkley in Lyon County. The monument notes no other tales. "Vandals stole a bronze plaque off it," said Odell Walker, a local historian and author.

The plaque was ultimately recovered. It belongs to Friends of Cobb's Battery, a group that takes care of the monument, which sprouts from neatly mowed grass just off Kentucky 295 near the little lakeshore community of Kuttawa.

The United Daughters of the Confederacy erected the memorial in 1931 to honor Major Robert Cobb's field gun battery, one of the most famous artillery units in the Rebel Army of Tennessee.

For years, knee-high grass, scrubby trees and underbrush masked the marker from motorists. In its heyday, the memorial overlooked the Kuttawa Mineral Springs, a well-known local spa.

"The UDC put the marker here so more people would see it," Walker said. But the springs disappeared in the 1960s when the Army Corps of Engineers built Barkley Dam across the Cumberland River and created the lake. Hence, the Cobb monument was all but forgotten. Even so, Cobb and his cannoneers—part of the Orphan Brigade—were remembered for bravery in several Civil War battles.

Cobb recruited his six-gun battery in his native Lyon County in 1861. Supposedly, the monument stands where he and his men left for the war. Later in the conflict, Cobb's cannoneers named three of their guns for wives of Orphan Brigade commanders: "Lady Breckinridge," "Lady Buckner" and "Lady Helm."

Cobb was still a captain when he and his gunners received their baptism of fire at Shiloh. "Capt. Cobb…unfortunately lost most of his horses and two of his pieces, but is represented to me as having fought with great courage and skill," reported Colonel Robert P. Trabue of the Fourth Kentucky Infantry, the brigade commander at Shiloh.

Until the war ended in 1865, Cobb's Battery provided potent firepower for the Confederacy. But the battery's legacy is partly literary, too.

Cobb's nephew was author Irvin S. Cobb, born in nearby Paducah. "Robert Cobb certainly helped inspire Cobb's writings about Civil War veterans, especially in the Judge Priest stories," said Anita Lawson, a Cobb biographer.

STILL WAITING FOR THE WHISKEY BOAT

Old-timers swore that there was a worried look in the stone soldier's eyes.

"He's facing forward, but his eyes are supposedly looking up the Ohio River," William Talley said. "They used to tell the story that the soldier was afraid he might miss the whiskey boat."

There is no other statue in Kentucky like the buff-hued limestone warrior who faithfully guards the Lewis County Courthouse in Vanceburg. He is a Yankee.

"The only Union monument south of the Mason-Dixon Line erected by public subscription except in cemeteries," explains a state historical society marker next to the memorial.

Talley, who taught psychology at McGill University in Montreal, Canada, but summered in Vanceburg, said that Lewis County was staunchly Unionist in the Civil War. Even so, not everybody appreciated the twenty-foot county seat memorial on whose base is chiseled, "The war for the Union was right, everlastingly right, and the war against the Union was wrong, forever wrong."

Talley added, "The same man who told me about the soldier waiting for the whiskey boat also said there was this woman in town—he called her an unregenerate Confederate—who would shout 'Hurrah for Jeff Davis!' every time she walked past the monument."

Sentry-like, the soldier stands, musket at the ready. He is perched atop a slim sandstone shaft raised to honor "the bravery and patriotism of our soldiers who lost their lives for the preservation of national unity, 1861–1865."

Talley said that the Vanceburg war memorial is even rarer than the historical marker notes. "That part about 'except in cemeteries' is a bit misleading. There are other Union monuments in Kentucky and the South but they are in national cemeteries where Union soldiers are buried."

Looking for the whiskey boat?
Photo by the author.

The Lewis County Monument.
Photo by the author.

Several Confederate memorials sprouted on courthouse lawns and elsewhere in the Bluegrass State following the Civil War. Never mind that Yankee soldiers from Kentucky outnumbered Rebels by about three to one.

"But after the Civil War, the old Confederates got control of state government and exerted a lot of influence," said Kentucky historian Thomas D. Clark of Lexington. "The Confederate influence in Kentucky was stronger after the war than during the war."

Even so, deep Union sentiment persisted in Lewis County. Two decades after the war, a local committee was organized to collect money for the monument to the county's fallen heroes. "I've never run across anything saying how much it cost, but there were probably quite a few small contributions," Talley said.

When the memorial was unveiled in 1884, there were many surviving Union veterans in the county. Old records credit Lewis County with 917 enlistments—including 4 African Americans—by January 1, 1865. Few Lewis County men put on Rebel gray.

Carved on the Vanceburg monument is the same verse that greets visitors to Arlington National Cemetery:

On fame's eternal camping-ground
Their silent tents are spread,
And glory guards with solemn round
The bivouac of the dead.

The lines are from Theodore O'Hara's famous poem, "The Bivouac of the Dead."

The Kentucky-born O'Hara was a Civil War veteran himself. But he might have objected to the words on the Vanceburg monument about the Union cause being "everlastingly right." The poet was a staff officer under Rebel general John C. Breckinridge.

MORGANTOWN MONUMENT MEMORIALIZES THE BLUE AND THE GRAY

Every Kentucky county furnished soldiers to both sides in the Civil War. But just one courthouse monument honors local blue and gray veterans.

"It may be the only one of its kind in the country," former Morgantown newspaper publisher Roger Givens said of Butler County's stone memorial to "Confederate and Union soldiers living and dead."

Most Butler countians marched off to America's bloodiest conflict in Union blue. A total of 571 enlistments—508 whites and 63 African Americans—were recorded through December 31, 1864. Rebel volunteers were considerably fewer.

Hence, the soldier atop the memorial is a Yank, resting on his rifle. Carved on the base of the monument are a medal of the Grand Army of the Republic, a Union veterans' organization, profiles of Lincoln and Grant and the names of some Butler County soldiers.

But also inscribed on the stone are the names of a half-dozen county Confederates and the profile of Rebel General Joe Wheeler. Included, too, is a roster of county Spanish-American War veterans.

An inscription on the monument notes that Robert V. Hunt of the Eleventh Kentucky Union Infantry was the "principal collector of funds" for

The Butler County Monument. *Photo by the author.*

the memorial; the project included ex-Union and ex-Confederate soldiers, according to Givens. "You could pay a few dollars and have a name put on the monument," he said.

Names include Granville Allen and Major Andrew Hamilton. Allen was reportedly the first Kentuckian—or at least first western Kentuckian—killed in the Civil War. Captured by the Rebels, Hamilton planned a famous escape from Libby Prison in Richmond, Virginia, the Confederate capital.

The monument's unveiling on May 30, 1907, made headlines in the *Green River Republican*. Publisher J.T. Rives, who fought on the Union side, was chairman of the monument committee.

Bearded, graying vets shook hands for photographers. "The old soldiers made a colorful background for a procession of children dressed in white and carrying flowers, who marched to form a circle around the monument," Grace Dabbs Dean wrote in a local history book. "While the two older girls slowly pulled the cord which unwound the bunting, the children placed their flowers at the monument's base." A band played "Tenting on the Old Campground," a popular Civil War tune.

Givens said that for many years Memorial Day celebrations were held at the monument. "Children would pick flowers, lay them on the monument and parade out to the cemetery to lay more flowers on the graves of Civil War soldiers."

"THIS FORGOTTEN AND NEARLY LOST GRAVE—THE GRAVE OF AN AMERICAN SOLDIER"

John Trowbridge likes reading about historical mysteries. He likes solving them even better.

Trowbridge's detective work got Union army Private Steven R. Kemper a new tombstone in old Lancaster Cemetery.

It began with a big bump. "Back in 2006, I got a call from Kevin Brickey, the cemetery sexton, who said he hit something while mowing the cemetery," Trowbridge remembered. "He said he thought it was just an ordinary rock."

The rock turned out to be the tip of a mostly buried military grave marker at least 104 years old. "It was lying flat, just below the surface of the ground, and in two pieces," Trowbridge said.

Both contained clues. "Emper," "Co. F" and "USCT" were carved into the larger chunk of white marble. A "t" was on the smaller piece. "Kevin and I both knew that 'USCT' meant 'United States Colored Troops,'" Trowbridge said.

Trowbridge also knew that the 1866 *Report of the Adjutant General of the State of Kentucky, 1861–1865*, contained the names of all Kentuckians known to have fought in the Union forces. "Through process of elimination I finally found who I thought was our man—a private in Company F, 114th Regiment, United States Colored Troops," he said. "The 't' was from 'Steven.' The 'emper' was 'Kemper;' 'Co. F' was 'Company F' and 'USCT' was the 114th.""

Even so, Trowbridge sought more proof. He discovered it in old census records. "In the 1870 census, I found Steven Kemper, age fifty, male, black, born in Maryland, working as a farm laborer in Lancaster."

The clincher was Kemper's service and pension records from the National Archives and Records Administration in Washington, Trowbridge said. "They showed that Kemper joined the army at Camp Nelson on June 18, 1864."

Trowbridge added that the 114th Regiment was an infantry outfit that was based at Camp Nelson and Louisa, the Lawrence County seat, until January 1865, when it was sent to Virginia. "The 114th was involved in the siege of Petersburg and was present at Appomattox Court House on April 9, 1865, when Lee surrendered to Grant," Trowbridge said.

Lee's capitulation effectively ended the Civil War. But the 114th stayed on garrison duty at Petersburg and nearby City Point until June 1865. The regiment mustered out after it was dispatched to south Texas to patrol the Mexican border against the troops of Emperor Maximilian I.

Honorably discharged in 1867, Kemper returned to his wife and daughter in Garrard County. Steven and Paulina Kemper reared another son and daughter.

"His time in service took a heavy toll on his health," Trowbridge said. "Eventually he became totally disabled and could no longer work." In 1888, the federal government granted Kemper a twenty-four-dollar monthly pension, which he received until his death in 1902. He was eighty.

Trowbridge doesn't know how or when the old soldier's grave marker was broken. "But through the years, it became covered with soil and almost completely disappeared until Kevin ran over the part of it sticking out of the ground. He had no idea the marker was there."

A new, Civil War–style grave marker was ceremoniously placed on Kemper's grave in 2007. Members of the Twelfth United States Colored Artillery (Heavy)—a reenacting group—served as an honor guard. Also, thanks to Trowbridge, Kemper's name was added to the National African American Civil War Memorial in Washington.

"Few records have survived that help tell Steven Kemper's story," Trowbridge said. "Yet we know he fought for his freedom and the freedom of his family and others held in slavery and for the preservation of our country. Now our generation and future generations can look upon this forgotten and nearly lost grave—the grave of an American soldier."

"Perhaps, a Ball from Some 'Vile Gun' Laid Him Low While He Was Taking a Lonely Stroll in the Woods"

They were heroes to their Kentucky Confederate comrades in arms. A Yankee cannonball killed one at the Battle of Shiloh in 1862. "I can never forget the seeming anxiety depicted on his countenance when we were getting shelled," a survivor remembered.

But the slain one's name is evidently unknown. The other was reported missing in Georgia in 1864 after he had been wounded. He was remembered only as Frank.

Frank's fellows described him as "faithful." Furry and four-footed would work, too. He was a dog. So was the Shiloh casualty.

Both canines made it into history. Twenty years after its death, the Shiloh dog was featured in an article in the *Southern Bivouac*, a Confederate veterans' magazine. Frank's story is in Ed Porter Thompson's *History of the Orphan Brigade*, which was published in 1898.

Just a pup, the Shiloh dog was adopted by a soldier of Company H of the Fourth Kentucky just before the bloody battle. "It seemed that the whole North had suddenly concentrated their stock of powder and iron and were determined to plow us up and turn us under," reports the *Southern Bivouac* story, which had no byline.

Company H sprawled on the ground, hoping to escape the deadly rain of exploding cannon shells. "The dog sat there, and...it seemed the missiles shook his ears by their close proximity to his head," the article noted. "This little long-eared puppy remained near his master, till the piece of iron ended his existence."

Frank missed Shiloh. He was captured with Company B of the Second Kentucky Infantry and the rest of the regiment at Fort Donelson. He shared his outfit's fate in a prisoner of war camp until the Second Kentucky was exchanged for Union captives.

In battle, Frank viewed fallen soldiers "with the eye of philosophers," wrote Thompson, an Orphan Brigade veteran. "The close observer might have discovered something of pity in his glance, and a half-consciousness that the poor man was dead, or in agony, and that he could not help him."

Frank, according to Thompson, met a "fate 'unknown.'" Frank's captain wondered if "some admirer of his species laid felonious hands upon him, and carried him captive away; or, perhaps, a ball from some 'vile gun' laid him low while he was taking a lonely stroll in the woods."

In any event, Thompson wrote, Frank "long shared with the men the privations of inclement season, scanty fare, and hard marching and the perils of the field…[On] almost all occasions, he seemed to partake of the spirit of the men.

"If the conflict was obstinate, Frank was silent and dogged. If the men shouted at the onset, or cheered when the ground was won, Frank barked in unison."

A "Man Wholly Without Fear, as Brave as Julius Caesar"

History doesn't exactly square on what really happened the day "Pud" Diggs died at the end of a hangman's rope in Murray, the Calloway County seat. Diggs, a Civil War guerrilla and outlaw chieftain, was executed on or about October 20, 1867.

Just before the trap was sprung, a shot rang out. The crowd fled in panic, fearing that Diggs's gang had come to rescue their leader.

Raymond Story of Murray said that his father witnessed the execution and claimed that a drunk in the Murray Cemetery, about a mile away, fired the shot. Two history books suggest that it was a prankster in the crowd. Either way, Diggs went to his doom after order was restored.

Diggs, from nearby Paris, Tennessee, bossed a pro-Confederate band that preyed on Union soldiers and pro-Union citizens in the Civil War. The gang would ambush small groups of soldiers and rob and murder men, women and, it was said, even children.

Diggs continued his criminal career after the fighting stopped. But his sins found him out. He was arrested and charged with murdering George Miller, apparently a Calloway County deputy sheriff. Found guilty, he was sentenced to hang on the court square.

A large crowd gathered to watch. Jailer John Churchill and his deputies had Diggs on the scaffold when the shot was heard. Story said that the culprit was a local boozer who had just arisen from a long, alcohol-induced slumber in the graveyard. "He decided to try his pistol at a target," Story explained. "That's when somebody shouted, 'The gang's coming' and everybody started running."

The Story of Calloway County, 1822–1976 by Dorothy and Kerby Jennings notes that a young man named Ed Ryan put the crowd to flight. The authors quoted John McElrath Meloan who said that Ryan "in the spirit of fun and deviltry fired his pistol."

Either way, everybody scattered for cover, except jailer John Churchill, a "man wholly without fear, as brave as Julius Caesar," according to Meloan. He stood by Diggs, single-barreled shotgun at the ready. "When the cause of the excitement was learned the crowd again assembled and poor Diggs who stood unmoved through it all, was successfully dropped to his doom," Meloan also said.

Ryan indeed fired his handgun as a joke, according to *Oklahombres*, the autobiography of E.D. Nix, a Calloway countian who became the first U.S. marshal of Oklahoma Territory. Nix claimed that he came to the hanging when he was a child.

But Nix said that Ryan stirred up more than the crowd. "At the crucial moment, just as the trap was about to be sprung, he raised to fire his gun and his hold slipped," Nix wrote. "As the gun discharged, he fell through the thick branches, knocking a hornet's nest to the ground."

Ryan crash-landed on a woman's neck. Meanwhile, the angry insects swarmed on the spectators, punishing several people and triggering another stampede, according to Nix. "Next day Murray resumed the peaceful routine of county-seat life although a few of the village's leading lights, whose stings were most inconveniently located, did not appear in public for a few days," Nix added.

"World War II Was Going On and People Had Their Minds on that and Not Some Old Civil War Cannon"

A Civil War relic hunter's dream was hidden below a forty-foot dirt bluff at Columbus-Belmont State Park for more than fifty-five years.

Eddie Roberts's cannon. *Photo by the author.*

That dream came true for Eddie Roberts. It took him fourteen years and two tries. But the retired schoolteacher unearthed a 7,545-pound Civil War cannon that toppled off the Mississippi River bluff in a 1943 landslide.

The old ordnance is back in the park.

The iron-barreled, Model 1829 Navy thirty-two-pounder gun was buried forty-two feet deep in the dirt. "We dug for three days before we found it," said Roberts, who lives near Clinton, the Hickman County seat. The state park is located in Hickman County.

Early in the Civil War, the Rebels strongly fortified Columbus. They dug deep trenches, planted 140 cannons—mostly atop the bluffs—and blocked the river with a heavy anchor and mile-long chain. Confident Confederates dubbed their bastion "the Gibraltar of the West." Like the anchor and short section of the chain, the cannon Roberts found was a featured attraction when the park opened in the 1930s.

He started hunting for the big gun in 1984. He dug unsuccessfully for it in 1991. He hit paydirt in 1998 thanks to excavating equipment furnished by Tim Schwartz and his son, Jason.

Many people believed that the cannon was a Confederate orphan, abandoned when the Rebels retreated from Columbus in March 1862. "But when the Yankees occupied Columbus, they used the town as a shipping point for captured Confederate cannons," Ross said. "They were shipped in and out of Columbus from all over. All we can say for sure is the lost cannon was here in 1865 when the war ended."

Ross inspected the gun shortly after it was recovered. "U.S." is plainly stamped on the barrel. A smoothbore cannon designed for shipboard use, the gun was cast in 1839 by Joseph McClurg, William Wade and Company at Pittsburgh's Pennsylvania Penn Foundry, also known as Fort Pitt Foundry, he said.

"McC. W. & Co. P.P.F." is stamped on the left trunnion and "1839" on the right. Trunnions are cylindrical projections on either side of a cannon barrel that hold the gun on a carriage.

Ross said that the cannon's discovery was "the most significant event for Columbus park since it opened." There were vain searches for the cannon at least two other times, said John Adams, a longtime park manager.

Tim and Jason Schwartz furnished two track hoes and a bulldozer for the earth work. The larger track hoe pulled the cannon from its deep grave. The Schwartzes scraped out a hole forty-two feet deep, twenty-four feet wide and forty feet long to help Roberts find the cannon. While the barrel survived the cave-in, the gun's one-ton oak carriage did not.

Unearthed, too, were several broken timbers and heavy metal straps used to fasten the carriage together. The excavators also found the carriage's smashed wheels.

Crews from the Civilian Conservation Corps—one of President Franklin D. Roosevelt's New Deal programs for fighting the Depression—built the gun carriage to exact Civil War specifications while they were helping construct the state park.

The cannon's demise had been little noted nor long remembered. Roberts read about it in a 1984 article published in the *Paducah Sun*. The story sparked his cannon quest. He had little to go on. According to most accounts, the bluff slide was in 1942. Ross discovered it was in 1943.

Roberts thinks that he knows why nobody tried to retrieve the gun when it was lost. "World War II was going on and people had their minds on that and not some old Civil War cannon," he suggested. "They just didn't bother with it."

Roberts extensively surveyed the area before he started digging. In 1991, the Army Corps of Engineers supplied a dozer and a backhoe. "They dug down about twenty-four feet," he remembered. "We didn't have any luck. Then my permit to dig ran out and that was about it."

Unknown to Roberts, the last hole he had dug was on top of where he would find the cannon seven years later. "We were just not deep enough." He used a powerful metal detector called a magnetometer to pinpoint the cannon in 1998.

A few people gathered on the riverbank to watch the unearthing of the cannon. Roberts was the first to lay hands on the muddy iron barrel after Tim Schwartz scooped it out with the track hoe. "Through all those years, he never lost faith he'd find it," an onlooker said.

Bibliography

Allen, Hall. *Center of Conflict*. Paducah, KY: Paducah Sun-Democrat, 1961.

Campbell, Given, Captain. "Memorandum of a Journal, Kept Daily during the last March of Jefferson Davis." Washington, D.C.: Library of Congress, n.d.

Collins, Lewis, and Richard Collins. *A History of Kentucky*. Covington, KY: Collins and Company, 1882.

Coulter, E. Merton. *The Civil War and Readjustment in Kentucky*. Chapel Hill: University of North Carolina Press, 1926.

Cozzens, Peter. *The Battles for Chattanooga: The Shipwreck of Their Hopes*. Champagne: University of Illinois Press, 1996.

Craig, Berry. "The Jackson Purchase Considers Secession." *Register of the Kentucky Historical Society* (Autumn 2001).

———. "Long Search Ends with Discovery of Thirty-two Pounder." *Columbiad* (Winter 1999).

Davis, William C. *The Orphan Brigade: The Kentucky Confederates Who Couldn't Go Home*. Garden City, NY: Doubleday & Co., 1980.

Donovan, John T. *The Catholic Church in Paducah, Kentucky*. Paducah, KY: Young Printing Company, 1934.

Duke, Basil W. *History of Morgan's Cavalry*. Cincinnati, OH: Miami Printing and Publishing Company, 1867.

———. *Reminiscences of General Basil W. Duke*. Garden City, NY: Doubleday, Page and Company, 1911.

George, Henry. *History of the 3rd, 7th, 8th and 12th Kentucky, C.S.A.* Louisville, KY: Dearing Press, 1911.

Grant, Ulysses S. *Personal Memoirs of U.S. Grant*. New York: Century Company, 1903.

Harper's Weekly

Harrison, Lowell H. *The Civil War in Kentucky*. Lexington: University Press of Kentucky, 1975.

Harrison, Lowell H., and James C. Klotter. *A New History of Kentucky*. Lexington: University Press of Kentucky, 1997.

Henry, J. Milton. *The Land Between the Rivers*. Dallas, TX: Taylor Publishing Company, 1976.

Hickman County Gazette

Jennings, Dorothy, and Kerby Jennings. *The Story of Calloway County 1822–1976*. Murray, KY: Murray Democrat Publishing Company, 1980.

Johnson, Adam R. *The Partisan Rangers of the Confederate Army*. Louisville, KY: G.G. Fetter Company, 1904.

Jordan, Thomas, General, and J.P. Pryor. *The Campaigns of Lieut.-Gen. N.B. Forrest, and of Forrest's Cavalry*. New Orleans, LA: Blelock and Company, 1868.

Kleber, John E. *The Kentucky Encyclopedia*. Lexington, KY: University Press of Kentucky, 1992.

Lexington Kentucky Statesman

Louisville Journal

McClellan, George B. to President Abraham Lincoln, May 30, 1861. Lincoln Papers, Series I. Library of Congress.

McDowell, Robert Emmett. *City of Conflict: Louisville in the Civil War 1861–1865.* Louisville, KY: Louisville Civil War Roundtable, 1962

Meacham, Charles M. *A History of Christian County Kentucky from Oxcart to Airplane.* Nashville, TN: Marshall and Bruce Company, 1930.

Memphis Appeal

Memphis Avalanche

Neuman, Fred G. *Paducahans in History.* Paducah, KY: Young Printing Company, 1922.

New York Times

New York Tribune

Nix, Evett Dumas, as told to Gordon Hines. *Oklahombres.* St. Louis, MO: Eden Publishing House, 1929.

Noe, Kenneth. *Perryville: This Grand Havoc of Battle.* Lexington: University Press of Kentucky, 2001.

The Official Records of the War of the Rebellion. Washington, D.C.: War Department, 1880–1902.

Perrin, W.H., J.H. Battle and G.C. Kniffen. *Kentucky: A History of the State.* 8th ed. Louisville, KY: F.A. Battey and Company, 1888.

Prentice, George D. "Legislative Document No. 26 Response of the Adjutant General of Kentucky to a Resolution of Inquiry in Regard to Federal Enrollments in the State, Made to the House of Representatives Wednesday March 1, 1865." *Kentucky Legislative Documents, 1863.* Frankfort, KY: George D. Prentice, State Printer, 1865.

Rothert, Otto H. *A History of Muhlenberg County.* Louisville, KY: John P. Morton and Company, 1913.

Russell, William Howard. *My Diary North and South.* Boston, MA: T.O.H.P. Burnham, 1863.

Shannon, Jasper B., and Ruth McQuown. *Presidential Politics in Kentucky: 1824–1948.* Lexington: Bureau of Government Research, College of Arts and Sciences, University of Kentucky, 1950.

Tarrant, Eastam. *The Wild Riders of the First Kentucky Cavalry.* Louisville, KY: Press of R.H. Carrothers, 1894.

Thomas, Edison H. *John Hunt Morgan and His Raiders.* Lexington: University Press of Kentucky, 1975.

Thompson, Ed Porter. *History of the Orphan Brigade.* Louisville, KY: Lewis N. Thompson, 1898.

Townsend, William H. *Lincoln and the Bluegrass: Slavery and Civil War in Kentucky.* Lexington: University Press of Kentucky, 2009.

Wallace, Lew, General. "The Capture of Fort Donelson." *Battles and Leaders of the Civil War.* Vol. 1. New York: Century Company, 1887–88.

Warner, Ezra. *Generals in Blue.* Baton Rouge: Louisiana State University Press, 1964.

Wiley, Bell Irvin. *The Life of Billy Yank: The Common Soldier of the Union.* Indianapolis, IN: Bobbs-Merrill Company, 1951.

Wright, T.J., Captain. *History of the Eighth Regiment, Kentucky Volunteer Infantry.* St. Joseph, MO: St. Joseph Steam Printing Company, 1880.